Heaven to Eden

(A play in rhyming verse for reading
enjoyment, movie animation, stage,
and opera)

By
Fikre Tolossa, Ph.D.

Strategic Book Publishing and Rights Co.

Book Design/Layout by Kalpart. Visit www.kalpart.com

Strategic Book Publishing and Rights Co.
12620 FM 1960, Suite A4-507
Houston TX 77065
www.sbpra.com

For information about special discounts for bulk purchases, please contact Strategic Book Publishing and Rights Co. Special Sales, at bookorder@sbpra.net.

ISBN: 978-1-61204-864-2

Library of Congress in-Publication Data

Table of Contents

Introduction

By Flora Williams

Dear reader:

This is an unusual Introduction to an unusual book. I am a Rabbi based in Charlotte, North Carolina. I possess an MA degree in creative writing. I am a published author of five books of poetry. I have been a Television Producer, "Blow the Trumpet", for the last 24 years in the same city. I am interested in and read literature, ancient history, religion and philosophy. I came across the work of poet-playwright, Dr. Fikre Tolossa, *The Hidden and Untold History of The Jewish People and Ethiopians* by sheer miracle. I saw his book on line without being guided by any one and without knowing anything about the author. He was born in Ethiopia and has lived for the past 25 years in the Bay Area of San Francisco. He earned his MA in creative writing in 1978 from the reputed Gorky Institute for Literature, Moscow, with the mark "Excellent" for his creative works in drama, poetry and prose. He was conferred upon a Ph. D.degree (Magna cum Laude), by the University of Bremen, Germany, for his special dissertation titled,*Realism and Amharic Literature,* in which he compared and contrasted his native literature with those of Russian and West European literature.

After I read *The Hidden and Untold History of the Jewish People and Ethiopians*, I was left in utter astonishment by the style of the author and the originality of the information enshrined in that small, yet unique piece. That book answered all the questions that used to puzzle me all those years pertaining to Melchitsedek King of Salem, Patriarch Abraham, Jethro the Ethiopian, the high priest of Median and the father-in-law of Moses, King David, and a number of biblical and historical facts shrouded in mystery and undocumented in the Holy Bible. I didn't waste time to get in touch with the writer. Ever since then, I have discovered Dr. Fikre Tolossa has written more than one book. *Heaven to Eden* is volume I of two books. The sequel is entitled *Promise Fulfilled*. He has composed more than 20 stage and screenplays three of which have been performed in Ethiopia. His very first play, *The Coffin-dealer and The Gravedigger*, has been staged with a great resonance in Berkeley and Oakland, California. It has been featured in Ethiopia since 1976 with brief intervals.

He has produced a movie, "Multicolored Flowers", a coming-of-age film with dramatic undertones and overtones. He himself wrote the screenplay of this movie in English, directed it and acted in it. He has published two books of verse in the German language. His German poems have been recited by German actors over Radio Bremen, Germany; and a German composer has honored him by composing music to his lyrics and performing them in public. Dr. Fikre Tolossa has appeared in anthologies with international poets and Nobel laureates. He is also included in *Encyclopedia of African Literature.* He has been professor of literature, creative writing, philosophy and liberal arts subjects in Germany and here in the United States. He speaks four languages: German, Russian, English, and his native Amharic. He has numerous unpublished works including books of verse in Amharic.

I had the opportunity to read some of his historical articles and lyrical poems in English, which are all profound and original. My greatest surprise came when he shared with me his unpublished dramatic epic in rhyming verse entitled, *Heaven to Eden,* reminiscent of the masterworks of our greatest poets—Dante, Goethe, and John Milton. But then, poet Fikre Tolossa being an Ethiopian, the descendant of Emperor Ethiop, who was the son of Melchizedek, King of Salem and High Priest of the Most High God to whom Partriarch Abraham bowed in reverence and paid tithes, he had and still has access to a vast library of information on divinity and the creation of the world unavailable to these European poets. As such, it is no wonder if his work is replete with divine information absent in their works. It is the same information that was available to Moses when he lived with and served his Ethiopian father-in-law Jethro, the High Priest of Median, who was himself the descendant of Melchizedek. Furthermore, we shouldn't be amazed if he has transcended subliminally beyound their scope, given his rich spiritual background and his personal spiritualiy.

His note to his book spoke to my heart and alerted me that I was about to experience a revelation of something unexpected. The following line leaped into my heart, "***The story takes place at a time of timelessness when God was all alone before He created any celestial and living beings***"

I decided to write him via Face Book my impressions of his book spontaneously, as I flipped through the pages. Please take these spontaneous impressions as an introduction to his book, instead of the usual carefully-worded and crafted introduction to a book, since these impressions are true and impromptu.

They are the following as they flowed without any editing:

Dear Chosen Vessel:

I have been in a quiet place. As I read the pages, I was transported to a special realm. In all the books I have read, plays, poems, and prose works of great writers, I was never transported this way to hear the plans and discussions of the Father, Son and Holy Spirit. The Holy Bible has been the only book that has lifted me beyond myself. The other books have been like ladder steps that prepared me to get to this book so that I can hear the plans of the Father, Son, and Holy Spirit from the beginning. There have been debates about the Trinity: How can the Son be God? Clarity and understanding to this question are conveyed in this work. Your dramatic piece brought me to heaven and provided a way for me to hear the plan of the Creator and the purpose of man being created in his image before the Garden of Eden. Surely, you brought such clarity and understanding to the question people may have about the Trinity. I reached the end of the first ten pages as if I had been moving along a perfect road, no bumps. Your writing captured my heart and never let go. I was so moved that I could not respond right away. I had to meditate. You brought me to heaven and caused me to share in the plans of the Creator and the purpose of man being created in his image. I am still in the pages. I hope that I have said enough to let you know. We need your writings, plays, books, dvds. We are waiting. I thought about Psalm/Tehillim 87 and the Messiah when I was reading.

Let me begin by saying this: I could not talk after reading these pages. I was so astounded I just could not get back to you before now. A perfectly set stage of order, transition and transforming... Lives will change through this writing. These are my feelings...A HUSHED SILENCE CAME OVER ME. I remember saying, now I understand Genesis 1:26 "Let us make man in our image." You really brought us to the beginning and allowed us to participate in the planning of Our Creator for us, His children. It is so remarkable how you remind us that earth will be the place for His birth.

I thought about the *Secrets of Enoch,* chapter 30:10-15 10. [Friday]. On the sixth day I commanded my wisdom to create man from seven consistencies: one, his flesh from the earth; two, his blood from the dew; three, his eyes from the sun; four, his bones from stone; five, his intelligence from the swiftness of the angels and from cloud; six, his veins and his hair from the grass of the earth; seven, his soul from my breath and from the wind.

11. And I gave him seven natures: to the flesh hearing, the eyes for sight, to the soul smell, the veins for touch, and the blood for taste, the bones for endurance, to the intelligence sweetness [enjoyment].

12. I conceived a cunning saying to say, I created man from invisible and from visible nature, of both are his death and life and image, he knows speech like some

created thing, small in greatness and again great in smallness, and I placed him on earth, a second angel, honorable, great and glorious, and I appointed him as ruler to rule on earth and to have my wisdom, and there was none like him of earth of all my existing creatures.

13. And I appointed him a name, from the four component parts, from east, from west, from south, from north, and I appointed for him four special stars, and I called his name Adam, and showed him the two ways, the light and the darkness, and I told him:

14. This is good, and that bad, that I should learn whether he has love towards me, or hatred, that it be clear which in his race love me.

15. For I have seen his nature, but he has not seen his own nature, therefore through not seeing he will sin worse, and I said after sin what is there but death?

I LOVE YOUR WORK!!!!!!!!!!!!!!!!!!!!!!!!!!!!!!!!!!!!

I will just keep writing to you as things come to my mind.

3/21, 2014,1:58pm.

Dear Dr. Tolossa:

Now I understand about the word "luck." In your wonderful introduction to *Heaven to Eden,* you inform us that this play is a fictional work of art with Biblical outlines. Further, that you are using poetic license to dare to be different in your poetic expressions of presenting this amazing revelation of the plan of God before creation took place. Utterly astonishing is that, truth is merely set forth in a fictional frame, but you and I know truth's anointing transports the individual who is blessed to read this incredible work of art.

I can only describe the "AUTHOR'S NOTE " by using an example of a surgeon who prepares to perform a major operation. He makes sure his staff and tools of his trade are in place. Everyone must harmonize and work as one to ensure that the operation is successful...And so it is with the introductory note to this dramatic work that stands out as a pioneer beckoning to us to read this magnificent work. The history and background was flawlessly knit together in a beautiful tapestry. I had no questions after reading your note.

Your writing is so anointed by the Spirit of God that I was immediately captured by your style of writing. The rhythms in the writing and the rhymes provided an undertone setting so that I could actually hear the Father, Christ and Holy Spirit speaking, sharing and discussing their plans for mankind. The rhythms of the rhymes would change and not all have exactly the same ending sounds and yet they worked perfectly. The rhythms were a transporter of sorts??? (Not sure I got this right, but I know how I felt when reading your work). The vivid fresh, new descriptions in the play, "**Humans are like drops of water leaving their sea as if forever in the form of vapor and rain, ultimately turning into a river**..." Wow! "**Let me now explain to you planet Earth and the rest...whose models I keep in this space I call 'life's nest.'**" So much in this work of art illustrates that a master builder is behind it alive and active. It grabs the spirit-heart, and all five senses work in unison to convey the meaning.

Sharing the plans with the angels and showing them the models that had been designed demonstrated Our Father's teaching about working as a team. Although Christ knew what Lucifer would do, he still shared the plan with him.

Hearing the plans about creating man and seeing the models through the eyes of your writing filled me with overwhelming joy. I felt special as I read about the plans for mankind. Earth became outstandingly special as the plans manifested that this would be the place where the Messiah would be given birth. We are so loved that a plan was put into operation at the beginning of creation. I thought about Psalm/Tehillim 139:14 I will hallel You; for I am fearfully and wonderfully made: marvelous are your works; and that does my being know full well.

This is a play that draws one closer to the Creator, Christ and the Holy Spirit. I know that we were there with them as they made plans for our lives and how each of us would be presented in this world. This play expands our knowledge of history and the Holy Bible. Furthermore, it reveals to us that God has created 100 worlds including Earth. It also throws light on the UFO (Unknown Flying Objects) phenomenon, which has been a mystery to many of us. Although the frame *Heaven to Eden* is fictional, truth speaks in it loudly. Any way, you know all this. I state all this just because you asked me how I found your work.

I hope I have said enough, to convey to you how blessed I have been to read your work. Yes, I read *Heaven to Eden*, as I received it. I will read it again. Give me a little time and I will give you more feedback. Your writing creates a hunger for more of your work.

I am still praying for your already published book, *The Hidden and Untold History of the Jewish People and Ethiopians,* to help bring in more finances. I believe this book has been sent into the world to help make a way for *Heaven to Eden.* Many of our people are searching for the Truth, but have not been connected to a person like you who has the Truth.

Thank you for allowing me to have the privilege of reading your amazing work of art.

Peace, blessings and contentment.

In conclusion, Dear Esteemed Reader, let me say a word about his unique style and the significance of his work.—

Genere wise, a screenplay in rhyming verse for movie, the stage, opera and reading enjoyment, in and of itself, is innovative or even novel. Dr Fikre Tolossa's work flows in a style all his own. He is a pioneer trailblazing a pathway for others to follow in expressing the truth of the straight and narrow road by employing an extraordinary musical language. The breathtaking imagery of his work expressed in rhyming verses that we, the native speakers of English have long forgotten, the sounds and smells in his creation, as well as the new vehicle by which he conveys a truth unrevealed to us by any poet in the past, are the evidence that this work has been anointed and appointed by God. Indeed, the rhyming endings are a total surprise to us because of the unusual way he uses words. As a matter of fact, he is breaking a new ground and expanding to a new territory in the literary world.

The poet's portrayal of heaven and the models of the first human male and female anatomy God had designed in heaven before the days of creation, compel us to appreciate the beauty and grandeur of heaven, and of the human body. The meaning of life and the reason for existence are laid out vividly. The description of 12 of the 100 habitable worlds God has created is astounding. We are transported, transformed, and transfigured by this work. If you are looking for the hitherto untold occurrences in heaven and paradise before and after the creation of angels, the physical universe, man, as well as the Garden of Eden, read this book; and you too, will feel its transforming power and the unfathomable Designer.

Last, as far as I am concerned, Dr. Fikre Tolossa is not a mere poet. He is a philosopher as well; because, even though the issues he address are presented in verse, they are profoundly philosophical. His editor is right in categorizing his work as philosophical.

AUTHOR'S NOTE

It all started when, out of curiosity, I tried my hand at translating Goethe's *Faust* and Dante's *The Divine Comedy* into Amharic, the working language of Ethiopia, and one of the oldest languages in the world with its own unique alphabets. After I translated a few pages from *Faust* in the original German and the English translation of *The Divine Comedy* whose original Italian I was also able to compare and contrast with the English version as far as the rhyming scheme and the wording were concerned, I decided to stop translating and write my own books. As I had been preoccupied for a long time with the same subjects these two classical poets dealt with, I thought it would be fair to myself to write my own books first and translate theirs last, if I ever decided to do so. Bearing this in mind, I boldly launched my own project and wrote two books one after another—*Heaven to Eden* and *Promise Fulfilled*.

Both volumes are based on *The Holy Bible*, which contains only sixty-six books, the *Ethiopian Bible*, which has eighty-one books, and the Ethiopian book of creation entitled, *Djan Shoa.* The latter book, *Djan Shoa* (called *The Book of The Wars of The Lord* in the English version of *The Holy Bible*), predates *The Holy Bible.* The Prophet Moses admits the existence of *Djan Shoa* in Numbers 21, 14, naming it as *The Book of The Wars of The Lord*. This book is supposed to have descended to the Ethiopians from Enoch via Noah. Moreover, I have used *The Lost Bible* and my own understanding of the scriptures, as well as my poetic fantasy, to compose *Heaven To Eden* and *Promise Fulfilled.*

Regarding *Heaven To Eden*, I didn't copy the Bible verbatim to reproduce it. I simply selected verses and chapters that served my purpose. Indeed, I used my imagination where details were absent or latent in the Bible, applying fully my poetic license. In other words, this work and the other volume are nothing but fictional works of art with Biblical outlines.

In this first volume, the story begins in heaven at a time when God is all alone, having yet not created celestial beings. He then decides to create angels to glorify Himself, share His life, make Himself be known, and have them as companions and servants. It depicts the fall of the rebellious angels first and that of man later on when God forms humans and the physical universe.

Indeed, I have been preoccupied ever since I was a teenager with the question of death, creation, God, the meaning of life, the origin and destination of the soul, humanity's ultimate destiny, as well as virtue and vice or good and evil. I attempt to address these issues in this present book and the one that succeeds it.

According to my review of the literature, there is no any other poetic, dramatic work that deals with the situation of God before and immediately after creation in heaven of angles, cherubs, and the physical universe in such a manner as this book does. John Milton, in *Paradise Lost,* which he produced about 375 years ago, recounts the rebellion of some of the angels against God in heaven but doesn't portray and show the process of the creation of angels and their rebellion. I portray and show the process of their creation, rebellion, and ultimate fall. Poets Dante and Goethe dealt with different aspects of the same themes and problems of free will, sin, condemnation, hell, and the Devil, which I too tackle in my own way. Dante did this 700 years ago and Goethe 170 years ago. And here I am, a twenty-first-century man from Ethiopia, dealing with the same questions from my own perspective because they are universal and eternal.

John Milton, in addition to his own account, narrates the story of the rebellion of the fall of angels through the mouth of Archangel Raphael, who shares it with Eve in the Garden of Eden. *Heaven to Eden* takes it a step further, dramatizing it. Also, Milton's works are narrative (epic). Mine are dramatic epic, like Goethe's *Faust,* if Faust could be so considered. In terms of volume, mine is the reverse of his. My *Heaven to Eden* is about the size of his *Paradise Regained*, whereas, my *Promise Fulfilled* is either longer or the same size as his *Paradise Lost.*

There are also stylistic and structural differences. Milton employed free verse, deeming English rhyming scheme to be unsuitable for epic narration. I rhyme in English, though I am not a native speaker of it. I learned English at school as a second language. Usually I write in Amharic and translate my works into English at times. This book was directly written in English though I had composed the beginning of the story in Amharic before deciding to write it in English for the world at large. In undertaking boldly the task of rhyming in English, essentially a foreign language to me, I hope I have proven John Milton wrong for stating that English was not suitable to rhyming epic works, which may have been correct only in his own time 375 years ago. Since his time, English has grown to be an international language, enriching itself with new vocabularies and idiomatic expressions that lend to the rhyming I am able to do today.

I believe that elevated subject matters such as God, life, death, eternity, evil, and good should be written in an elevated language and style, such as poetry and rhyming verse. This is the reason why I wrote this book in such a fashion. Instead of bending myself to the will of the English language, I have made it bend to my will through the rhyming style I employ.

In this and the other volume, I sometimes deliberately rhyme words that usually are not rhymed with in English such as "and" and "bend" or even "and" and "end". I do so partly as a way of experimenting with the language and partly for fun.

Fine works in prose have been composed in English by writers whose native tongue was not English, including Joseph Conrad. Still, my dramatic rhyming verses were not as easy as prose to compose. According to an Ethiopian proverb, "He who has used the weapon at his disposal in a battlefield is not considered a coward." I guess this proverb applies to me.

As stated earlier, with this book, in my own humble way, I have attempted to address the most important metaphysical questions man in general, and philosophers in particular, have been posing in all ages: God and the meaning, origin, and purpose of reality and existence.

Furthermore, I have portrayed in a poetic image the wonder of the human anatomy that people take for granted, so that they can reexamine their own superb bodies and become startled by them, besides seeing their Maker in their intricacies. I have also thrown a fresh light on sex and the reason for sexual attraction as well.

As for heaven, the Bible doesn't detail what it looks like. It seems that we know more about hell than heaven. So, I have fantasized what heaven might possibly look like. Also, the Bible doesn't give any account of God's life when He was alone in eternity before He created angels.

Therefore, my story begins at a time when God was alone and "lonely." Likewise, the scriptures do not seem to document the process of the creation of angels, nor even of the universe.

When it comes to the creation of the world, according to the scriptures, God simply said let there be this and that, and everything came into being. I contend that He had made models of everything out of His energy, which was pure energy, before He spoke them into existence, even as an architect first and foremost designs and makes models of his edifices before he builds them for real. Finally, the scriptures don't reveal how Lucifer enticed and won over the hearts of the other angels to join him in his rebellion against God. I have tried to fill this gap.

My forty plus years of experience in writing Amharic poetry and drama definitely prepared me to compose these books in English. Most native speakers of English stopped writing poems that rhyme with the introduction of blank or free verse to English literature over a hundred years ago.

There was a time (in my teens) when I experimented by writing in free verse in my mother tongue. In fact, I published a few poems in the national papers in Ethiopia that resonated when I was a high school student. Later, I reverted to writing the classical, rhyming poetry. Now every poem I write in Amharic rhymes in accordance with my own style. So, I transferred this skill to English poetry. In this connection, you will note that I come from a country with a very rich tradition of poetry where both laymen and scholars, common folks and royals, and soldiers and farmers, composed poems when under emotional situations to express their innermost feelings, be it orally or in writing.

In my country of birth, Ethiopia, the Ethiopian clergy left a legacy of books that deal with a wide range of important subjects such as cosmology, astrology, geology, literature, arts, theology, history, medicine, government, law, and biography.

The longest and best part of the *Book of Enoch*, probably the oldest book in the world, was found in Ethiopia. The *Book of Maccabees III*, the *Book of Manasseh*, and *Metsehafe Kuffale (The Book of Jubilee*, a book ascribed to Moses) are a part and parcel of the Ethiopian Bible, as they exist only in Ethiopia. As I said earlier, the three books mentioned above and the *Book of Enoch* are listed as integral parts of the Ethiopian Bible (the Old Testament) with the other books known in the West as apocryphal.

Surprisingly, these extra four books and the rest of the fourteen books don't contradict the sixty-six books of the Western Bible. On the contrary, they complement them and provide details missing in them. Indeed, they enrich the five books ascribed to Moses by providing information absent in the five books, including Genesis. For instance, the *Book of Genesis* in *The Holy Bible* doesn't mention that Adam and Eve were formed in a place called Elda near the earthly Garden of Eden (which was a replica of the Heavenly Paradise) and placed in the Heavenly Paradise located in the Third Heaven. The Ethiopian book of creation found in *Djan Shoa* does give all these details, making it clear that Adam and Eve were created in Elda and placed in Paradise, which was located in the Third Heaven (which Saint Paul had seen, without being sure whether spiritually or physically, according to his own account). Jesus promised on the cross to the good robber that He would see him in Paradise the same day after they met their death, proving that Paradise was not on the physical Earth. In my second volume, *Promise Fulfilled*, I have attempted to prove that Elda was located in Ethiopia. The reader can check that out when the second volume sees the light of the day.

It seems that the original *Djan Shoa* was written in the Suba language. The Suba language spoken in Babylon was destroyed by God while the Babylonians were building the tower of Babel contemptuously, besides worshiping King Nimrod as God. However, it is reported that Suba has survived among some priests and among some minority ethnic groups in Kenya and Tanzania. As far as the written Suba is concerned, I have the Suba alphabets and a dictionary of the Suba language in my possession. The *Djan Shoa* was most likely passed on to Noah by his grandfather, Enoch, before the Flood, and brought out of his Ark afterwards along with other books including *The Book of Adam*, which is now in the possession of Ethiopians.

It is written in *Djan Shoa* that God created seven heavens and placed in them one hundred worlds. We are in the First Heaven. There are sixteen worlds, including ours, within our heaven, four of which are lifeless. I will describe this in detail when I deal with the creation of the universe in this drama. By Moses' own admission, as I said earlier (Numbers 21, 14), he was familiar with our book that predated the Bible, *Djan Shoa (The Book of The Wars of The Lord)*. This means he had read it while he was living with his Ethiopian father-in-law, Jethro, the High Priest of Median, and later Emperor of Ethiopia. In *Djan Shoa*, it was stated that God created one hundred worlds including our own. Nevertheless, for reasons obvious only to himself, Moses chose to describe in his book of creation only the formation of this world, even though he knew that God had created more. He probably thought that it was enough if his people dealt with the world they knew and lived in.

Although Ethiopian scholars and clergymen have known of the existence of one hundred worlds for over four thousand years, Western scientists are just beginning to suspect and theorize the possibilities of the existence of other worlds and intelligent beings outside our solar system. They speculate about parallel universes and even claim that they have detected using telescopes new worlds with solar systems. It was obvious to the Ethiopians that intelligent beings from worlds they knew by names such as Memros flew to Earth in spacecrafts (UFOs) to live here and intermarry with humans before they were destroyed by God about six thousand years ago for polluting humans and the planet with evil deeds. I write about this in this drama because I feel that it is very important for people to be aware of the fact that life doesn't exist only on our planet. God has placed life on one hundred worlds if not in more, and the glory is His. For the last fifty years, some individuals have narrated their encounters with UFOs. Others have even confessed that they were abducted by them. I suspect that these extraterrestrials are engaged in secret missions at present, one of which is genetic engineering to enhance their biological makeup and ugly looks, by mixing their genes with ours. If these extraterrestrials decide to come out openly in the near future and claim to be gods that have created us in a laboratory on account of their highly advanced technology, many people will be shocked and confused about God and their religions since they had thought that life existed only on Earth. Should that happen, they would have to blame only themselves, because God has never told them that He created only one world called Earth and that there is life only on Earth. Therefore, it is to minimize this shock and doubt that I indicate in this work that God has created at least a total of one hundred habitable worlds, according to the ancient Ethiopic document stated above.

Our Ethiopian book of creation has a chapter on dinosaurs even though it calls them behemoths since that is their original name. The word "dinosaur" is a recent invention. According to our book, behemoths (dinosaurs) existed side by side with humans but most were hunted down and annihilated by the hungry giants that were born when the extraterrestrials, the so-called sons of God, mated with our women. These giants, whose heights "reached the skies," were constantly hungry because of their size, hunted the dinosaurs in groups, and ate them all up. God then drowned the giants in the flood of Noah for unleashing violence and perversion on Earth. I have dedicated a few lines concerning this in my *Heaven to Eden*. Our book also mentions that Adam and Eve served and worshiped God for seven "God years" (2.5 million years according to man's concept of time) before their fall.

The Book of Enoch details how the fallen angels, misusing the secret knowledge they had acquired on the Mount of God when they were in heaven, taught men witchcraft, besides perverting them in so many ways. It identifies these angels by name, such as Azazel, Semazya, and Annanel, and relates how God had them bound and confined in spiritual pits of fire because of their evil deeds. Some scholars suggest that Moses quoted the *Book of Enoch* when he wrote about this and the giants briefly in Genesis. I concur with them since Moses had access to this and other ancient writings in his association with his Ethiopian father-in-law, Jethro, the high priest of Median who had a bunch of them, as I indicated earlier. I was fortunate and privileged in that I was able to tap into these and the other rare books and access fresh information, which I used poetically in this and the succeeding volume.

As far as religion is concerned, Ethiopians practiced both Judaism and Christianity for the last three thousand five hundred years, unlike other nations that were converted straight from paganism to Christianity. As a matter of fact, Ethiopians had worshipped the God of Adam and Noah long before Judaism came into existence. Jethro the Ethiopian was a high priest who believed in and worshiped the God of Adam and of Noah. He was the descendant of Melchizedek, King of Salem, to whom Abraham paid tithes and by whom he was blessed before and after he battled with four kings to free Lot and his household. As aforementioned, Moses had access to all the ancient books in the possession of Jethro when he was his apprentice, assistant, and shepherd for forty years before he was called by God to set His people in Egypt free. The eunuch that Apostle Philip baptized and converted to Christianity was an Ethiopian who had practiced Judaism before his conversion to Christianity. Ethiopia claims to possess the Ark of the Covenant containing the tablets in which God wrote the Ten Commandments with His own fingers and handed over to Moses.

According to the Ethiopian *Gospel of St. Marher* and the memoir of his father, Ethiopian King of Egypt Amanatu Tetnai, Joseph, Mary, and Jesus found refuge in the Ethiopian colony of Egypt, which was Northern Egypt. Southern Egypt belonged to the Romans from whom Jesus had fled. Prince Marher was the son of King Amanatu Tetnai. Jesus and Marher were neighbors and playmates. Later, when Jesus was twenty-two years old, He traveled to Ethiopia with Prince Marher and his cousin, Prince Dimas, and lived there for three years, preaching, healing the sick, and raising the dead. He left Ethiopia for Israel when He was twenty-five years old, after appointing the two Ethiopians as His apostles and representatives in Ethiopia. Dimas was burnt at the stake forty years later by jealous Ethiopian Levites. According to King Amanatu's account, it was twelve Ethiopian kings (two of which were his father and older brother), the descendants of Melchizedek, King of Salem, who took presents to Jesus when He was born in Bethlehem, and not some dubious wise men from the East. St. Mathew wrote about these "wise men from the East" without giving their exact number, after he journeyed to Ethiopia and met some of them there. Being instructed by Jesus Himself to go to Ethiopia to see His Ethiopian friends, five or six of His Jewish disciples, surely Mathew, Bartholomew, Mark, Thomas, and Nathaniel, went to Ethiopia. They shared the Holy Communion with the Ethiopians and baptized many of them easily since the legwork of believing in Him had already been done by none other than Jesus Himself. In my second volume, *Promise Fulfilled*, I detail the life of Jesus in Ethiopia for three years.

Unlike the Church in Europe, which was divided into hundreds of parts in the wake of the Reformation, the Ethiopian Tewahdo Church has remained intact to this day despite its conflicts in the past and internal doctrinal differences. The Ethiopian Church is deeply entrenched in the Gospels. It has its own unique mass, hymns, and songs that reflect both Judaic and Christian elements absent elsewhere in the world. As such, it shouldn't be a surprise to anyone that I have written books of this magnitude and nature.

By training I am a creative writer and a critic. I never studied theology in a seminary like John Milton did. Even though I have had some divine, visionary encounters, which impacted upon me profoundly, my knowledge of the scriptures emanates purely from my reading of the Bible and literatures related to it. I have also read the *Koran* carefully and compared and contrasted it with the Bible. Moreover, I understand the essence of Buddhism.

Dear reader, if some of my lines in this and the other work don't correspond to the *Holy Bible* that you know, and this stirs in you a feeling of uneasiness, it is because mine is a work of imagination based on the scriptures, and not a replica of the *Holy Bible*, as I indicated earlier. As a matter of fact, 90 percent of this book is my own poetic fantasy. Be that as it may, I promise to furnish the reader with a new insight into the understanding of God and the creation of the Universe, which will enhance and enrich the reader's spiritual knowledge, if the reader is ready for it.

I wrote most of this book in 2004. However, I held it back from publication while composing the second volume, *Promise Fulfilled*, so that I could revert to it in case I decided to make some changes and modifications. I am glad I did this. I did indeed go back to it to make some changes in light of the new information I obtained after I wrote it four years ago. Now, I will publish volume one and two together. God willing, depending on the outcome of these two books, I anticipate writing a few more on this thread, even though I don't promise that they too, would be in rhyming verse, as this will be too cumbersome to undertake.

This piece could be read as a dramatic literature, performed on the stage as a play and opera, and featured on a screen as a motion picture—as animated film, to be precise. I found screenplay writing to be convenient to developing my play. Which is why you will see some words in capital letters and screenplay terms such as "Angle" "Ext. (exterior)" "Int." (Interior), "Fade in," "Fade out," etc., in this and the other book. Please ignore these and focus on the drama.

Finally, a note to the camera crews and directors that might film this screenplay: I know you can feature this play as a movie, if you so desire, since it has all the elements and characteristic features of a screenplay. I have given you the general directions. However, I don't feel like dwelling on minute directing details such as *"close ups, medium shots, long shots, three shots, povs,"* etc., lest I bar the spontaneous flow of the play trying to focus on such a directing parlance. I will leave this for you as you might choose to shoot it from different angles and in different ways than I suggest when you are in the actual shooting scenes. This holds true also for those music directors that would like to present my play in the form of opera.

Fikre Tolossa, PhD
Vallejo, California,
September 27, 2008

EXT. HEAVEN. AT A TIME OF TIMELESSNESS.

"FATHER GOD," AS WELL AS "THE WORD," LATER KNOWN ON PLANET EARTH AS "JESUS CHRIST," "THE MESSIAH," AND "THE HOLY SPIRIT," (THE THREE GODHEAD THAT WOULD BE CALLED "TRINITY" BY CHRISTIANS DURING THE CHRISTIAN ERA), ARE SITTING ON THREE THRONES DECORATED WITH GOLD AND PRECIOUS STONES. THE THREE THRONES THEMSELVES ARE PLACED ON YET ANOTHER GRAND, AWESOME THRONE IMPLYING THEIR BEING ONE, AND AT THE SAME TIME THREE. FATHER GOD IS IN THE MIDDLE, THE "WORD-CHRIST" IS ON HIS RIGHT, "THE HOLY SPIRIT" IS ON HIS LEFT. THEY ARE ENCIRCLED BY A RAINBOW LIGHT, WHICH DENOTES THEIR UNITY DESPITE THEIR INDIVIDUALITY.

THE STORY TAKES PLACE AT A TIME WHEN GOD IS ALL ALONE, BEFORE HE CREATES ANY CELESTIAL AND LIVING BEINGS, INCLUDING ANGELS. SINCE THE "WORD" WAS POPULARLY CALLED "JESUS CHRIST" AFTER HE BECAME FLESH (HUMAN), WE WILL IDENTIFY HIM IN THIS PLAY AS "CHRIST" FOR THE SAKE OF DRAMATIC CONVENIENCE UNTIL HE IS BORN ON EARTH TO BE CALLED "JESUS". OTHERWISE, HE SHOULD HAVE BEEN CALLED "THE WORD" IN HIS HEAVENLY STATE. WHEN "THE THREE" SPEAK IN UNITY, I WILL IDENTIFY THEM AS "TRINITY" FOR CLARITY. EVEN THOUGH THEIR FACES AND STATURES ARE IDENTICAL, I WOULD LIKE TO HAVE THE BODY OF FATHER GOD PORTRAYED BLUE, OF JESUS, WHITE, AND OF THE HOLY SPIRIT, YELLOW, TO DISTINGUISH THE THREE FROM EACH OTHER WHEN THE PLAY IS DRAMATIZED ON THE STAGE AND THE SCREEN. THEIR ATTIRES TOO, SHOULD BE OF DIFFERENT COLORS.

FATHER GOD
The three of us have existed together in oneness for eternity.
We're alone in our abode, which has been tranquil for infinity.
We dare not say we're Lord of Lords loudly,
Nor do we declare we're King of Kings proudly,
Because there're neither lords nor kings,
Though we're over and above all things.

There's nothing exciting in our life forever and ever,
Nothing dramatic for which to aspire or endeavor,
No grief in our heart with which to measure our joy,
Nothing fantastic in here to make us say, "Ahoy!"
Nothing with which to while away our endless time,
Our dwelling's empty, though splendid and sublime.

HOLY SPIRIT
Verily, you spoke what's in my heart as a load! . . .
To break the silence and lonesomeness in our abode,
But most of all, to share our life unconditionally
And generously, and to offer our love additionally,
Let's create celestial beings, majestic and tough,
Called angels and cherubs out of fiery stuff.
Then, surely, our life will transform radically forevermore
Changing our thoughts and feelings unlike the days of yore.

CHRIST
A fine idea, Holy Spirit!
Oh, I like it every bit,
And would endorse it!

HOLY SPIRIT
Not only will they partake of our Life and break our loneliness,
They'll forever serve us, worship us, and aspire for our holiness.

CHRIST
We know we exist forevermore, but there are none who know
We exist. If we create beings, our glory will show and glow,
And radiate itself to all, and they'll recognize our presence,
Even though they'll find it hard to fathom our divine essence.

FATHER GOD
Let's then create them cheerfully at this very hour!
However, I wonder with or without free will power.

CHRIST
If we create them without free will and the ability to decide
To do wrong or right, to be against us or to be on our side,
If they don't have the choice to love us or hate us indeed,
If we don't grant them the freedom to heed or not to heed
To our words and commandments, they'll be lifeless bound
By our will, mere toys that we maneuver and drive around.
We want every angel to be nothing but a living entity,
With intelligence and emotions, lasting for eternity.

Holy Spirit gazes into the future with His right hand raised above His eyes.

HOLY SPIRIT
What if they abuse their free will and rebel?
In fact, seeing the future, I can already tell,
If we grant free will, some will surely rebel!

CHRIST
Let's bestow free will taking a chance. When some rebel,
We'll waste them away in a Lake of Fire worst than hell.

HOLY SPIRIT
Since we'll create them out of our energy,
When they go out of control in sinful orgy,
As they can't go out of existence eternally,
Indeed, we will dissolve them infernally.

FATHER GOD
I foresee most of them won't make any strife,
They'll love and serve us for granting them life.
In fact, most will worship us; they won't forsake
Us at all. Hence, we should grant life for their sake.

HOLY SPIRIT
Let's not deny existence those that'll be loyal
Because of those that will commit betrayal,
And fall into the pit of shame and disgrace,
And we cast them someday out of our face.

FATHER GOD
(to Christ)
It'd be good if you become the active agent representing
Us all, when we generously create henceforth everything.
Verily, from now on, you should be the middleman
Between us and those we'll create in every time span.

CHRIST
I feel honored to do so. This is my life's greatest call!
I'll gladly accept it and play for us this fabulous role.
May I go ahead then, and create their mold?

FATHER GOD & HOLY SPIRIT
Yes, fantasize them any way you like. Be bold
In your fancy. Feel free to create them with exuberance, dignity,
And bright mind, though some will choose to be filthy for infinity.

CHRIST
I'll make them exquisite and eternal out of pure fire,
With the ability to feel, reason, sing, and play the lyre
In our praise. Then, I'll divide them into legions,
Assigning archangels to lead in different regions.
In fact, I'll make one of them the chief of all,
Very charming, graceful, powerful, and tall.
I'll endow him with musical talent, unsurpassed beauty,
Brilliance of mind, fluency of speech, and unique ability.
For a while, he'll be our confidant covering our throne.
All angels must then obey him without groan and moan
Until the day of his fall, filled with contempt
And arrogance when he makes an attempt
To topple over our throne dreaming in vain
To be equal to us, causing unbearable pain.
Meanwhile, I'll create him perfect, out of flaming fire.
I'll adorn him with emerald, topaz, ruby, and sapphire.
I'll make him joyfully the wisest of the wise.
I'll establish him on our Holy Mountain, to rise,
To sit down, and to walk freely back and forth,
In the midst of fiery stones, down south, up north.
I'll make him flawless and our closest friend,
Till iniquity is found in him, sadly, in the end . . .

HOLY SPIRIT
And what a pain he'll cause, indeed!
He'll surely make our heart to bleed
When he entices our angels, stealing
One out of three, shamelessly dealing
In lies, cruelty, deceit, slander, hate, and treason,
Destroying himself and them without a reason.

FATHER GOD
Let's not look only at its negative side.
The positive side will occur at the tide
Of his rebellion when the majority
Of angels triumph over the minority
Standing on our side defending our honor,
Transforming into joy our sorrow and horror,
Proving their unflinching loyalty to us forever,
Fighting the evil ones with selfless endeavor.

CHRIST
I'll call this wonderful chief of angels "Lucifer."
He'll illuminate the heavens and the atmosphere.
Yeah! He'll be a morning star, spotless and bright
As none, until his fall, crushed totally by our might.

FATHER GOD & HOLY SPIRIT
O, our Word, go ahead! Create on our behalf all and him. Our dream
Shall be real. The future is bright, however murky it may now seem!

*Christ makes instantly a BIG, COLORFUL WORKSHOP with His mind and creates in it
miniatures (models) of angels and cherubs out of His energy. He creates Lucifer's model
brighter, bigger, and more beautiful than the rest. He then shows them all to Father God and
the Holy Spirit.*

CHRIST
How do you like these models, aren't they great?

FATHER GOD & HOLY SPIRIT
They're superb! It's now time to create!

CHRIST
(to the models)
All of you models, grow big and be real right now! It's our will
That you multiply in number and the heavens fill ....It's our thrill!

*The models become real angels and cherubs with shining and glowing bodies as well as
wings, to the surprise and delight of the Holy Trinity. Christ writes on Lucifer in FLAMING,
GOLDEN LETTERS: "ARCHANGEL LUCIFER, CHIEF OF ALL ANGELS, SERVANT OF
THE MOST HIGH GOD."*

LUCIFER
(as if awakening from a long slumber)
Great is our God that has made us all something,
Creating us out of the void; yeah! out of nothing!

Fikre Tolossa, Ph.D.

Christ creates musical instrument such as FLUTES, LYRES, HARPS, CYMBALS, CESTRUM, and TAMBOURINES, and places them mentally in the hands of Lucifer and the rest of the angels.

Lucifer leads the angels in worship, singing and playing the instrument.

FADE OUT.

FADE IN:

After a period of time has elapsed in heaven since the creation of angels.

INT. IN A GLITTERING COURTYARD.

THE HOLY TRINITY
(sitting in their thrones)
Ever since we created angels, indeed our attitude
Has changed, we don't feel anymore our solitude.
We're now so busy with our wonderful angels like never
Before. They serve us obediently with such a great fervor.
They adore and love us affectionately,
Even as we love them passionately.
Their songs of praise are pleasant to our ears.
As things stand now, our angels have no fears.

They'll remain fearless till the day
Lucifer will turn evil and betray
Us. So far, we've created all these celestial beings.
It's about time now to contemplate physical things
And Beings. We'll create beings such as animals,
Of all sorts and classes including various mammals,
After making worlds to house the animals and vegetation,
We will create man as the crown and apex of our creation:
Rational, yet emotional and eternal, in our own divine image,
To rule over a world with a special privilege from age to age,
Till his tragic fall someday misled by vicious Lucifer
Forfeiting his power to him, compelling us to transfer
His privilege to rule the world to our adversary,
Until we, ourselves, then find it very necessary
To go down to Earth in due time and rescue man from evil,
From Lucifer's jaws, who'll then be called "Satan" or "devil."

FATHER GOD
When man falls trusting a creature than his own Creator,
He'll surely die physically, and worst of all, and greater
Than that, he will definitely die spiritually,
Being cut off from us because of sin actually.

HOLY SPIRIT
Since in our eyes, his motivation to reject our advice,
Unfortunately, is to be equal to us driven by vice,
He'll be as sinful as Lucifer for also committing treason,
And just like him, he'll lose Paradise for the same reason.

Unless we make a real atonement for his deplorable sin,
Like the angels that'll fall, he'll be a criminal: an assassin,
A murderer, traitor, thief, father of deceit, and liar.
And as such, he'll join Lucifer in the Lake of Fire.

FATHER GOD
When man commits high treason conspiring
With our enemy to be equal to us, aspiring
And desiring the impossible, he should be executed
Absolutely, and by no means shall he be acquitted.
Though we'll be a God of mercy most of the time,
Sometimes, we've to serve justice punishing for a crime.
Since we can't be partial, if we punish the vicious Satan,
For a crime, we've to do the same to man. This is certain!

CHRIST
Other than that, the process of creation should be fun.

FATHER GOD
Your idea of creation is exciting! Man will be our son.

HOLY SPIRIT
Go ahead our Word, create man's model any way you prefer,
Sharing our grand plan with the angels and even with Lucifer.

CHRIST
I'll surely be delighted to create the physical, visible things
And beings, as I was joyful when I created the celestial beings.
Since man will be the work of my own creation,
I'd gladly like to do for him also the mediation
To reconcile him back with us, to avert
His going to hell with Lucifer the pervert.
Instead of angrily annihilating the entire human race,
I'll die for every man that'd walk on Earth's surface,
If to serve justice, my death will suffice,
And if the two of you accept my sacrifice.

FATHER GOD
Accept we will, since your blood shall be most precious;
But it's horrible you'll die for man, who'll then be vicious.

CHRIST
Because I'll love man so much, I've to die in his stead.

HOLY SPIRIT
Loving, we'll love him too with our heart and head.
Since the world will be in need of a real savior badly,
Oh, our adorable Word, we will allow you to die, sadly,
So that whoever believes in you then shall never perish,
But rather live for eternity, thrive and forever flourish.

CHRIST
Since we know the fate of man ahead of time,
Using the stars as letters, we'll write his crime
And salvation in the heavens, drawing pictures with the stars, for man
To decipher both, and for us, to document there our redemption plan.

FATHER GOD
Besides heralding our redemption plan and telling a heavenly story,
Stars shall be time signs, direction guides, and expression of our glory.

Christ claps His hands. Lucifer enters, bows, and stands before Him.

LUCIFER
Yes, Almighty God and Lord!

CHRIST
The Three of us are in one accord
To create cheerfully and lovingly, physical, visible things
And beings, even as we created all you celestial beings.
Share the good news with the rest.
Gather them from East and West.

LUCIFER
Surely, my God, I'll do my best!

Lucifer leaves.

CUT TO:

INT: CHRIST'S WORKSHOP. DAY, AS ALWAYS IN HEAVEN.

While Father God and the Holy Spirit are watching Him, Christ creates out of pure light models of man, animals, solar systems with Earth and the other planets, worlds, stars, waters, plants, etc. He talks to them when He finishes modeling.

CHRIST
Look at them, aren't they fantastic!

FATHER GOD AND HOLY SPIRIT
So nebulous, so fluid, yet somewhat realistic
And solid in texture, while being even elastic!

Lucifer comes back, bringing with him all the archangels, many other angels, seraphim and cherubs.

CHRIST
(pointing out the human models)
These are the models of our creation.
They'll be the source of our elation.

All the angels, seraphim and cherubs look at the models, particularly the human models, with fascination.

LUCIFER
(dumbfounded)
They'll also be a reason for our jubilation!

CHRIST
These miniatures are actually entities or human souls
In embryo, who'll remain here till they receive our calls
To wear befitting physical attires on earth,
And undergo what'll be there called birth.
These are only our first group of souls, would-be people.
We'll continue to create souls until human beings triple
And quadruple in order to fill Earth forevermore,
Like the stars of heaven and the sands of seashore.
Since Earth will be too crowded to house and feed
All at once, they'll be born in different ages indeed . . .
We'll enliven these souls soon and permit them to live
With us here, growing in our knowledge until the eve
Of their birth on Earth, someday when the time is right
To part from us losing their heavenly memory, which might
Otherwise interfere with their earthly life hindering their progress,
Dividing their attention and causing sluggishness and undue stress.

MICHAEL
Lord, they're awesome! Could you please explain
How the models work, making it simple and plain?

GABRIEL
Yes, Lord, we're etching with curiosity.
They're complex despite their simplicity.

CHRIST
(pointing at the human models with a golden cane)
This is the mold of the future man, the apex and crown
Of Our creation, of darker complexion first, later brown,
Yellow, fair, and white as he undergoes changes in time,
Which will occur due to climatic conditions. The rhyme
Of the lyrics of our creation, he'll indeed be a royal baby
For whom you angels and cherubs will sing sweet lullaby.
We will honorably bestow upon him our divine quality,
And raise him above all our creation in terms of equality.
If he walks with us in conformity and harmoniously,
We'll shower him with our blessings continuously.
We'll give him power to rule over the Universe,
Anointing him to sing and praise us in verse.
Verily, this fabulous being, this lovely object of our adoration
Called "man," will be blessed from generation to generation.
We'll make his spirit most bright, dynamic, and immortal.
He'll be our conscious design, but by no means accidental.

He'll have a fraction of our emotions and reasoning power.
And surely, among our handiworks, he, only he, will tower!
And you, our angels, will guard man tirelessly in all ages.
And when the need arises, deliver to him our messages.
We'll share with him only a fraction of our love, for, if we put
Too much of our love in him, he'll explode and be utterly kaput.

LUCIFER
O! Praise be to our God who reigns in the heavens above,
And to man, who'll be down there, the object of His love!

All angels repeat the above couplets after Lucifer.

LUCIFER
(not so sure of what he states)
If it pleases our God to regard and honor man better
Than us angels, we will accept it. We won't be bitter!

All the angels repeat the same.

CHRIST
I'll place life in one 100 worlds, but my focus is on Earth,
Since it's on this special world that my own human birth
Will take place after Earth is filled with many people later
When the conditions for my birth become ripe and better.

I'll start the Universe with stars of red-hot matter,
And explode it and expand it slowly, but surely, later.
The stars whose models I've designed are now very small;
But in the distant future they'll blossom like flowers. All
Will stay in the heavens strong and won't crumble or fall
They'll begin small and grow, even as humans start small
and develop over the months and years to grow big and tall.
I like to begin with little things, actually,
Such as seeds, and let them grow eventually.
You may call these seeds the initial universe seeds,
For it is indeed like seeds that the universe breeds
Until I stop willfully its expansion,
After it accomplishes my mission.
In the far future, after the Universe expands, humans will call
This "The Big Bang Theory", when in knowledge they grow tall. .

Let me now explain to you planet Earth and the rest
Whose models I keep in this space I call "life's nest."
Take a look in here—these are 16 planets, a few moons, and many stars.
Man will see only eight that he will call Mercury, Venus, Earth, Mars,
Jupiter, Saturn, Uranium, and Neptune. All will revolve
Around a star called the Sun to gradually and surely evolve
Functioning perfectly and moving around their orbits, seeming frail,
Yet firm, attracting and balancing each other. They will never derail.
And with these fantastic stars we'll write on the Universe—
They'll be our poetic expression, indeed our shining verse.
Of course, Earth we'll adorn more than the rest,
For she'll be in the future man's awesome nest.
To this end, we'll make her shape oval rightly,
So that when the Sun shines on her brightly,
She'll cast a shadow which we'll call "night."
We'll call "daytime" the one that's bright.
The hot Sun will be day lamp, reaching its zenith at noon.
And for a night lamp, we'll create a yellow, mellow moon.
Verily, with the stars, we'll write the future at the right moment,
By treating as parchment the vast and magnificent firmament!
When we clothe these fluid planets and stars, for instance,
With matter, they'll be three dimensional of solid substance,
So that, the fluid and the solid, the spiritual and the material,
Are united into one, though it may sound surreal and ethereal;
Thus, one part becoming the reverse side of the other part,
Despite the fact that they seem to be detached and far apart—
Within the material Earth will be a spiritual Earth as a surprise,
Within the material Paradise will be latent the spiritual Paradise.

PHANUEL
Forgive me if I sound funny—these planets you'll set in motion,
Will they sit on some sort of columns, each having a cushion?

CHRIST
(chuckling)
Oh, no, I won't place them on columns of any sort,
I'll suspend them in the space without any support.

PHANUEL
It'll be awesome beyond description, indeed a miracle,
To see them running forever with no support in a circle!

LUCIFER
(concerned about man)
I'm getting more curious about this being
That you call man, who'll be Earth's king.
Lord, would you please describe him more?

Christ fixes His gaze on Lucifer for a second, knowing beforehand how Lucifer will damage man and God someday. Nevertheless, He decides to define man and describe his anatomy in detail.

CHRIST
Yes, I can't hide it—him I'll exceedingly adore.
Only he'll be my tender handiwork, therefore,
He'll have external and internal qualities and parts:
Body, spirit, and soul, or call it mind, when he starts,
And he will end up being more of spiritual entity,
As he matures in our knowledge to inherit eternity.

His physical body I'll adorn and clothe with flesh.
If he doesn't sin, he'll remain everlastingly fresh—
He'll be glorified and live without decaying for eternity
After his earthly sojourn, when he joins us in heavenly unity.
(pointing at man's model)
Man will have a head with brains in it of much
Benefit, neck, shoulders, chest, abdomen, such
Kind of torsos and feet. His head or mind will give out orders
To all the other parts of the body to do unthinkable wonders.
Even as you, dear Lucifer, are the Chief of Angels in actuality,
Man's soul is its chief, controlling his mind and body in reality,
Except that you, our Archangel, do not control
Our angels. You only play loyally a chief's role.

LUCIFER
(in his heart)
If man's soul controls man's mind and body, whoever can
Control the soul of man, can surely and easily control man.

The Holy Trinity reads the heart of Lucifer and looks at him sternly. He realizes this and feels embarrassed.

CHRIST
Man is our masterpiece, our priceless work of art,
Conceived in our mind and produced by our heart.
And if man seeks evidence for our existence,
He shouldn't look farther than his own essence.
(pointing at the anatomy of man as He speaks)
I'll protect his fragile but amazing brain with a hard helmet
Called skull, covering it with hair suitable for every climate.
I'll shape his ears in such a fashion so that they can
Receive sound, making it comprehensible for man.
I'll place his eyes under a protective forehead
High above, so that he could see far, far ahead.
I'll cage his most delicate organs inside a rib,
That will house all of them like a warm crib.
I'll attach the internal organs to numerous blood vessels
To nurture them. I'll strengthen the bones with muscles.
I'll interconnect each cell, muscle, vein, and sinew
With each other, to support one another and renew
Themselves when they get damaged because of much usage and age,
As long as man nourishes them with good food to repair the damage.
His feet will his entire body support,
And serve him as a means of transport
When he moves. In order to avoid stiffness in him,
I'll make joints in him, be it in his right or left limb.

SAKUEL
(pointing at the genital organ of man)
What's this, Lord God? If it was at the back,
I would've said, it's a tail. But it's not. I lack
The fantasy to understand clearly the exact function
Of this front tail-like thing. I'm lost at this junction.

CHRIST
(after laughing)
Oh, Sakuel, you're something! It's not a front tail.
It's a male's reproductive organ. Wait for the detail.
It can't function as intended if it's at the back. So, I don't
Want it at the back. The female organ too, is in the front.

SAKUEL
(pointing at the female organ)
Okay. I presume this is a female organ. It's plastered here securely as if
It was a leaf pasted on a cliff. The male one seems a bell hanging on a cliff.
Christ is amused. He smiles.

LUCIFER
Oh, my God! Being man is something to be envied and desired!
How lucky will man be! Verily, verily, he'll be highly admired.

RAPHAEL
(pointing at the breasts of the female model)
Lord, what are these papaya-like swellings hanging on the female? Must
They really be hanging seeming to be out of place like that on her chest?

CHRIST
(smiling)
These are breasts, which are milk makers and containers.
They're very necessary for the mother the baby to nurse.
However, the father might fondle it in lust being perverse.
An adult man might even be attracted to it getting so wild,
Acting like a milk-thirsty little baby, a breast-sucking child.

GABRIEL
(pointing at the butt of man)
Lord, I too am very curious—what are these things, which stick out
At the base of their backs? The female's is even bigger and stout.

CHRIST
They're their buttocks. They sit on them. They're padded
With flesh. Or else, their bones will pain them. I added
Them last realizing their importance. They're chairs, basically.
I shaped the woman's beautifully to attract the man physically.

GABRIEL
It's clever of you, Lord. It means, instead of carrying chairs around,
They can carry their butts and sit on them, be it on a rock or ground.

Christ and all the angels laugh.

MICHAEL
Lord, I have a quick question—
Trying to figure out the equation,
How are plants, animals, and man to continue as before?
Are you going to keep on creating them forevermore?

CHRIST
Good question, Michael, what a surprise!
Creating the same thing forever is unwise.
We'll create only once female and male of everything,
Placing seeds of their kinds in their innermost being.
They'll multiply and spread by themselves without alteration,
Passing on their seeds further from generation to generation.
We will set only once everything in the big Universe in motion,
And everything will run by itself forever in perfect locomotion.

MICHAEL
Oh, dear Lord! That's very smart!
My! My! . . . What a wonderful art!

CHRIST
Observe every model or mold I have in store.
Each model has its opposite part. Furthermore,
One can't be complete and exist without the other being active.
One is female, the other male; one is negative, the other positive.
I call this the principle of the unity of opposites. In order to be fair
And to guarantee their continuation, I've created everything in pair.
The plants, animals, and man are in perfect union.
Oh, no, I haven't left them alone without companion.
(pointing out a butterfly, flower and bird)
I design meticulously even the tiniest things
With devotion and love, because, this brings
Me indescribable joy. These tiny butterfly, flower, and bird share
The same pattern. Because I've designed each with a special care,
The butterfly looks like the flower; the flower resembles the butterfly;
The bird has semblance to both of them. The result I get when I apply
The principle of creativity with care and detail is such an alluring
Charm. I'll put some level of consciousness in them, so that during
Their life span, they'll recognize me not only as their Maker,
But also as the provider of their needs and their caretaker.
I create uniquely. Observe the butterfly, flower, and bird carefully—
Though the three have some semblance, each is unique to itself fully.

Christ leads His angels to models of fruits, picks up some, and discusses His design.

CHRIST
(holding each fruit as He speaks)
I'd like you to observe these fruits I use as samples.
I'll choose mandarin, banana, and walnut as examples.
Let's start with this mandarin. It has seeds and delicate

Fruits inside it. Its design is simple, and yet, it's intricate.
To protect and preserve its seeds, I have buried them inside
The fruits. And to protect wholly each fruit, I had to decide
To cover and wrap it meticulously and lovingly with a suitable skin
Or jacket, even as humans will wrap gifts later on. The banana is akin
To the mandarin when it comes to skin. The skin of a banana is long
And symmetrical in shape, covering its diameter and running along
Its length. The walnut has a shell, which is harder because
Its kernel is hard. So, I clothe every fruit with the right hose
Or coat. Likewise, I'll clothe the flesh of man with a skin to keep it wet,
Protect it from dust or germs, cool or warm the body and let out sweat.

RAPHAEL
Lord God, but all the fruits of heaven don't have such dresses.

CHRIST
Heaven's fruits are safe. Earth's will be full of calamities and stresses.

PHANUEL
O, Lord God, you're a wonderful dressmaker,
Besides being a superb designer and caretaker!

Christ smiles. The angels laugh.

CHRIST
I should add a thing—under the skin of the mandarin I've indeed
Stored sweet juice, under the banana, sticky fruit, and tasty seed
Under the walnut. It's for man I've so done. First, it's man I'll feed.
Sadly, man will be dumb and take all this for granted as if the fruits
Themselves created their covers and flavors and planted their roots.

RAGUEL
You said it rightly, O, Almighty God. It's indeed sad and a sign
Of dumbness. It's baffling why man won't see you in your design.

CHRIST
(after a pause)
I'll renew and replenish Earth now and then, to make life bright
For our beloved man, for the sake of his pleasure and delight.
I'll forever and ever make Earth rotate on her own axis
Once every twenty-four hours, in a steady practice,
And revolve her around the sun once a year for my own reasons:
To create time, and having created it, to spice it up with seasons,
Adorning winter with soft snow or rain showers,

Spring, with heaving grasses and dancing flowers,
Summer, with laughing skies and stars that quiver and twinkle,
Autumn, with fiery and golden leaves, which sparkle and crinkle.

GABRIEL
Lord God, how would this Earth function,
I mean in what fashion or course of action?

CHRIST
I'll make Earth totally dependent on the Sun above
For energy, climatic, and seasonal changes it'll have.
The Sun will provide plants with the energy they need
To sustain themselves regularly, as well as to interbreed.
So that the good Earth with her rich soil everyone can feed,
I'll pour down silvery rain on her from time to time, indeed.
I'll suspend the Sun at a particular point in space, away
From Earth, so that it won't burn or freeze her in any way,
For, if I place the Sun at a spot one bit lower or one bit higher
Than that, Earth will surely freeze with ice or burn with fire.
In other words, everything I design and create shall function
In order, beauty, musical harmony, rhythm, and perfection.

GABRIEL
Oh, my Lord, why do you place humans in a haven
Called Earth? Why don't you keep them in heaven?

CHRIST
Humans are like drops of water leaving their sea as if forever
In the form of vapor and rain, ultimately turning into a river
To flow through valleys and forests without border or margin
And drain back after a long sojourn into the sea, their origin.
Unfortunately and sadly, not all the drops will make it back home.
Some humans, because of free will, shall deliberately choose to roam
About elsewhere rather than return to their origin and heavenly home.
Giving man relative freedom, we've to test him by intentionally making
Ourselves invisible to him during his earthly life, to see if he's breaking
Our laws, and whether he'll believe in me without seeing me,
Since real faith is believing in something one doesn't see.
You angels don't need any faith at all to believe,
Because you see us every day, and to us you cleave.
Yet, if man seeks me with all his soul and mind mending his ways,
I will respond to his supplications and reveal myself to him always.
We've to allow man to be tempted on Earth to find out whether
He's worthy of joining us later in heaven for eternal life together.

Besides, we want to check out how humans treat and interact
With one another in circumstances where it is a must to react.
In other words, Earth will be a place of screening and purification
To determine the future of mankind. This'll answer your question.
Yes indeed, being invisible and seeming to be distant,
We'll monitor closely how man behaves at every instant.

RAPHAEL
What'll hold down men and animals to the ground,
So that they don't float in the air and fly around?

CHRIST
Clever question, Raphael. Something called gravity that I'll place
In Earth prevents men and animals from disappearing into space.

LUCIFER
Lord, you said, some human beings won't make it back
To heaven. How's that so? I'm puzzled and taken aback!

CHRIST
(fixing his gaze on Lucifer)
Some won't respond to our call,
Regrettably. They'll sin and fall.

LUCIFER
Lord God, it's hard for me to comprehend and fathom how such
Sort of beings would sin and fall when you adore them so much.

CHRIST
(shaking His head in amazement)
Oh, Lucifer! This will be evident to you in due time,
As you become the principal witness of their crime!

Lucifer is left wondering how on heaven he would be the principal witness of man's crime.

RAGUEL
Since we angels are neither female nor male really,
Neither negative nor positive, we can't tell actually
What's what. For instance, how does man breed?

CHRIST
Here's how, Raguel—remember I spoke about seed?
I'll place seeds in man and his other half—woman.
They'll have seeds called sperm and egg, which can,
When they join together, propagate other men and women.

RAGUEL
Amen, Lord, amen!

CHRIST
(pointing to the male and female parts)
Since you asked being so curious, look at the man's private part
And of the woman's. Nothing happens when the two are apart.
I'll put in man and woman a thing called "sexual attraction,"
Which pulls them towards each other in instinctive reaction,
Making them seek for their missing parts and fill them continuously . . .
Yes, their private parts will go into each other and fit in harmoniously.
It's a pleasure, which renews itself joyously again and again,
So that they can crave repeatedly and have it without pain.
At the climax of this pleasure they yield and release their seeds, which
Fertilize to be humans with ease, thus bringing immense ecstasy to each.
Look! Both the male and female organs can fit into each other well.
I've designed them precisely. They'll bind the two beings like a spell.
They will fit together exactly like a key and lock on a door.
This perfection and precision will last on Earth forevermore
In order to flung open the womb's gate
For conception, when a couple copulate.
(more to Himself than to the angels)
Sex is enjoyable and sharpens love if it's practiced in holy
Marriage. Sadly, humans will pervert it due to lust and folly.
(pointing again at the female private part)
This female part I'll adorn with hair that's straight or curled,
Shall be the gateway through which humans enter the world.

Since both male and female are made up of each other, neither
Of them is completely male or female. In order to live together
Harmoniously and understand one another to some extent, one should
Be the other's half. So, they won't be strangers to each other. It's good!
(singling out the womb of the female model)
In this bag way up here that l call a womb
I'll keep for nine months the being whom
The parents will call "child," so that it can be nourished
With life-sustaining food in there till birth, to be cherished,
No doubt equally by us and human parents alike,
Since it'll the hearts of God and man with joy strike.

Food is essential. The baby shares its mother's food through a chord.
When it grows, its mother's breasts make milk being in one accord
With its development. It feeds on milk until it grows teeth and adjust
To solid food. The teeth chew the food so that the stomach can digest
It. This way I will guarantee that the child has food for its survival.
Surely, everything will be ready on Earth for the child on its arrival.

MICHAEL
Lord God, what if man stops eating when he grows
Up; or hating to keep food in his stomach, throws
It up? How can he nourish his body then?

CHRIST
We'll create a recurring hunger in man when
He refuses to eat; lest he dies slowly for not taking
Food. Invoking a craving for food in him and making
His mouth water, we will compel him to gulp the food.
Thus we will be the one that force him to be in the mood
To move his lazy fingers to pick up and eat the needed food.
But foolish man would think it's he who wills to eat fruit or meat
Unless he chooses to starve to death, we prompt even his desire to eat.
So that man doesn't poison or infect his system, he should release
Toxic or wasted food. We will cause him to do even this with ease.

GABRIEL
What if he abuses food without any necessity.

CHRIST
Then he will die from obesity.

(pause)

Though parents feel they own a child, they'll safeguard God's interest
In reality, for God entrusts them to keep the child for Him like a trust.

(pause)

There'll be a parallel between a child and a ripe fruit that will be torn
From its mother tree. When a child becomes mature enough to be born
It'll push down its mother's womb in the same way a ripe fruit
Will push down to be detached forever from its branch and root
To grow up by itself and bring forth its own fruits turning to a tree
In its own right; to become independent and everlastingly free . . .
It's necessary for both baby and fruit to be separated from their origins
So that they can grow big, be self-sufficient, and thrive in different regions.

(pause)

PHANUEL
So, Lord God, this sexual attraction, according to your grand plan,
Is a coaxing for breeding, attracting, and gluing man and woman?

CHRIST
(after a laughter)
Surely, Phanuel! Reproduction is its synthesis,
After all is said and done in the final analysis.

(pointing at all the openings and organs of man)

Seven openings shall man have, this lovely, favored hunk
That we adore much—five on his head, and two on his trunk.
These two openings with sound receivers are called "ears."
They're designed to catch sound. It's with them that he hears.
These two openings over here are called "nostrils."
Through them he breathes and with air his lungs fills.
This hole is his mouth for which his chin serves as a seat.
With it, he speaks out his mind and is also able to eat.
His mouth is a piece of mill with teeth, which grind food;
And a tongue and saliva that mix it when he's in the mood
To eat food, to soften it, and send it down these tubes,
To these small and large intestines with these lubes,
Where it'll be processed, assimilated, and distributed
Through the veins to the cells and organs attributed
To the whole body, so that the good food would nourish it,
And the wasted, solid foods through this bottom hole exit.
This hole on his private part at the lower part of his front trunk
Will release the wasted liquid of whatever man will have drunk.
The genital parts of both sexes serve two ends: sexual pleasure
Culminating in reproduction, and waste liquid outlets in measure.
A woman will have eight openings for the same function,
Since she'll be different in emotions, feelings, and reaction.

URIEL
I'm flabbergasted, Lord! Man is a superb creature,
His nature is going to be different than our nature!

CHRIST
I'll make the human body from cells, tissues, and organs
That function in harmony everlastingly to serve man's
Needs, forming different systems, which would be very vital
As long as man lives, since, sadly, he'll choose to be mortal.

These are lungs, this is kidney, this is liver, this is heart.
Each has a function in collaboration with each other part.
The heart pumps blood; the lungs inhale and exhale air.
The kidneys and liver filter food as if they were a pair.
Blood is a transporter carrying food and oxygen to the cells
As it circulates through the veins in which it securely dwells.

The cells need food to thrive and flourish.
Man should eat food the cells to nourish.

This is man's eye that I designed for his sight.
It contains sophisticated cells, which detect light.
It has lens in the front and retina at the back wall.
They're made of cells that are very, very small.
These wonderful cells are close to many a nerve ending.
A picture is formed as the lens makes a light bending.
The nerve endings pick up signals to pass on to a nerve
Attached firmly to the brain for the brain to observe
Immediately the signals and interpret them and send away
A message to the parts of the body to react in a certain way.
Cells and organs are interconnected with veins and arteries.
And I'll make sure all of them have their own tributaries.
Each cell and each organ is so intricate and so sophisticated
That if I explain it in detail now, will be very complicated . . .
(showing man's limbs)
Look at each leg and each arm.
It's pretty! It has its own charm!

MICHAEL
(pointing at the joints)
Yes, but I don't comprehend why you did make
On the limbs these joints here and that break.

CHRIST
Without these joints, the limbs will be as good as a refuse.
As I said before, they'll be stiff and extremely hard to use.
(after a pause)
In time, we'll enliven man here in heaven so that he can be trim
enough to live with us till we fashion an earthly home for him.

GABRIEL
Speaking about man's eyes, when man is asleep, how would he protect
His eyes from harm, since during sleep, there's nothing he can detect?

CHRIST
(pointing at man's eyelids)
Even as lips are the doors of the mouth, his eyelids, which are the doors
Of his eyes, will protect them when he's sound asleep or when he snores.

GABRIEL
How can he shut them when he's sound asleep or when he snores?

CHRIST
He doesn't have to shut them himself. They're automatic doors . . .
I want man to understand that though his body may decay and fade
As a result of sin, he is the vortex of my creation, and designer-made.

Christ becomes sad.

Yes, I have designed man lovingly and meticulously.
But someday, some people will deny this ridiculously,
Speculating that men are accidental animals descending from monkeys.
They'd say this hating me their Creator, though men's anatomies are keys
To unlocking the existence of God and the mystery of creation.
God's haters will make up such misleading lies in desperation.

The angels feel His sadness.

LUCIFER
Humans that reduce themselves to monkeys denying
That you are their Creator would be indeed lying
A white lie. They must be dishonest, rebellious and blind spiritually,
If they lower humans created in God's image to animals, actually.

Looking into the future, Christ sees how Lucifer will use Charles Darwin, the speculator of the theory of evolution, to deny the existence of God.

CHRIST
A man called Charles Darwin will mislead many. Tragically, Darwin
Will reduce man, the apex of my creation, to an animal. But I'll win . . .
Just because he denies my existence, I don't go out of existence.
Woe betide those who follow him blindly without any resistance!
His falsehood will appeal to many for it excludes God from the picture.
As such, they'll think God won't hold them accountable in the future
For anything they'll do. So, they'll sin boldly living a life of perversions
And violence. But all will face me in the end to answer for their actions.
Verily, this deceitful snare will trap many. A fairytale called "evolution"
Will cause much calamity and bloodshed by kindling many a revolution,
Which will promise heaven on Earth to mislead the naive and to deceive.
Sadly, it is godlessness, havoc, and tyranny the reward men will receive.
Darwin's theory of evolution will be considered by the gullible a scientific
breakthrough. I will call it "the biggest deception of the age", which's terrific.
True scientists will discover me while examining the intricacies of my works.
Any scientists that fail to see me in my complex works are nothing but jerks.
Since it's I who created all things and gave them their first jerk,
A scientist or anyone that doesn't recognize this, is indeed a jerk.

The angels turn sad.

(pause)

SAKUEL
Lord, if you know ahead of time that Darwin would indeed
Do so, why would you allow him to exist and do evil deed?

CHRIST
There will be some humans that'll hate me being unfair
And irrational. To judge these, I'll use Darwin as a snare.

SAKUEL
What if some believe him considering him right and bright?

CHRIST
I'll judge them for making me a liar, considering him right.

(pause)
LUCIFER
Lord, can one female and another, and one male and another,
Produce a child, if they, being of the same sex, mate together?

CHRIST
Oh, no, no! I didn't design them to do that, of course.
Such an attempt would be a diversion from my course.
A female egg can be fertilized only with the sperm
Of a male. Here, my stand is clear and firm.
If I intend otherwise, I would actually design and create
Only female or male. My idea of opposite sex is great.

FADE OUT.

Eons of years pass by in heaven harmoniously, and evil starts to wax in the heart of Lucifer.

FADE IN:

INT. IN THE FIFTH HEAVEN. HALL OF WORSHIP.

Lucifer is leading the angels in worship, halfheartedly.

LUCIFER
(to himself)
I don't like anymore this repulsive tumult
Made by these stupid angels. And this cult
They all call worship is to me repugnant!
I wish I could stop it! Ah, I'm indignant!
I, Lucifer, will never have peace of mind till I enchant and compel
These idiots to praise and worship me, alluring them with my spell.
Yeah! With the same mouth with which they flatter
God, they must all praise me loudly as their latter
Day god, that has set them free from tyrannical existence,
Which, due to ignorance, they tolerate without resistance!
(flattering himself)
I'm second to God, but second is not first
Comparing second with last, second's worst.
I would rather be last than second to Him.
Either I'm first or none. Chances aren't slim
For me to be the first and last, to be Alpha and Omega,
I, Lucifer, the greatest of the great, the mega of mega!
I will gamble with my life; and am sure to win;
For, gambling and winning are inseparable twin.
But all the same, even if I lose completely and fall,
I'll win; since I'll be out of God's will and control.

FADE OUT.

FADE IN:

EXT. FIFTH HEAVEN UNDER A BLOOMING TREE.

ANGLE ON LUCIFER

Lucifer is standing in a pensive mood under the BLOOMING TREE.

Archangel Michael joins Lucifer.

MICHAEL
What's wrong, Chief, your demeanor's not the same as before?
I see that you've a sad countenance unlike the days of yore.

LUCIFER
Oh, Michael, those were wasted, naïve yesteryears,
When everything was sweet to my heart and ears.
There's bitterness in my soul now!

MICHAEL
(surprised)
But how!
Who's like you, O! Lucifer, even if all of us were put together,
Compared with you, we're nothing all but a worthless feather.

LUCIFER
Compared with you, yes, but compared with God, I must
Admit, beloved Michael, I am less than a particle of dust.

MICHAEL
You're almost second to God, what else do you want to achieve, Chief?

LUCIFER
I don't want to be second to none, though this sounds like a mischief.

MICHAEL
(terrified)
Lucifer, I don't really get that!
You want to be God or what!
Evil ambition has crept into your heart!
Better rebuke it now from you to depart,
Lest God and all angels get outraged, and on your face spit,
And you fall disgracefully for eternity into a bottomless pit!

LUCIFER
Oh, Michael, you've no idea about freedom.
It's the desire to be free, and this boredom
That I endure every day in submission and bondage
To God, chained to His cumbersome throne in this cage
Called heaven, guarding His innermost secrets that I share
With none, whose burden I can no longer tolerate and bear . . .
I'm sick and tired of praising
Him day in day out, raising
My voice, till my throat and tongue painfully crack,
Bowing and kneeling till it hurts my knees and back,
Yeah! Michael, it's this great unquenchable craving
For independence and liberty, which makes me raving.

MICHAEL
Lucifer, it's because you're thinking evil that you're in pain.
I feel no pain, for I serve my God lovingly again and again.
Our dear God deserves more than praise and worship
For all the things He has done for us in His Lordship.
Even if we stop praising Him, heaven's flowers and birds
Will praise Him loudly with sweet, reverberating words.
You're heading towards a destruction lasting for eternity.
Beware! Before it's too late, choke and kill your vanity!
We're all dependent on the grace of God. There's nothing
Wrong with this, since on Him depends our very being.
Even as the movement of a ship depends on its navigator,
The creature depends eternally on his Maker or Creator.
Only the Almighty Creator is ever self-sufficient and efficient.
The creature is needy, and by definition, eternally deficient.

LUCIFER
"Navigator" . . . "ship". . . where did you these words pick?

MICHAEL
The Holy Spirit made me these words speak . . . surely, you're sick!—
Even as the nature of plants makes them depend on soil and light,
All created beings depend on their Creator; and this is alright . . .
How dare you be so unthankful and unfaithful! . . .
Ah, Lucifer! How on heaven can you be so hateful
To such a generous God, who, with many gifts did enrich each
Of us, and elevated you to such heights none of us could reach?

LUCIFER
Trust me, Michael, and follow me,
I'll set you free, like you'll never be.

Later, I will make you the head of all the other
Angels. I'm now your boss . . . your chief, rather.
Henceforth, I'll make you my ally. All I ask when I set you free
Is to worship me like the rest of the angels in devotion and glee.

MICHAEL
(disgusted and angered)
I'll worship God only! Lucifer, get out of my face!
I do not respect you anymore, you're a disgrace!

Michael leaves Lucifer.

LUCIFER
(to himself)
If Michael's so dumb and stupid in such a matter,
The rest of the archangels won't be any better.
I'd rather entice the common angels and cherubs to conspire,
With false promise for freedom, setting their naive hearts afire.
Let God call it scandal, slander, betrayal ,or treason.
As far as I'm concerned, I have a justifiable reason.
Paying any price, I've to ascend into heavens' heaven.
I'll place my fabulous throne high above the stars, even
Above God and the angels. I'll sit on the Mount with pride,
On the most holy congregation on the farthest Northern side.
I, Lucifer, will ascend above the heights of the firmament.
I'll be like the Most High God, even if only for a moment,
And all angels have to worship me in adoration,
Praising me loudly, glorifying me in admiration.
What's the point of my being called splendid, mover-shaker
Wise, majestic, graceful, spotless, perfect, and wonder-maker,
If no one praises and worships me in adulation,
If I am not revered and praised in jubilation?

MOVING SHOT:

Lucifer moves away from the tree and meets Azazel, one of the most active angels.

LUCIFER
Azazel, my friend, how do you feel? How's life? Are you good?

49

AZAZEL
(surprised that Lucifer called him friend)
Did you call me friend? Glory be unto God, I'm good as I should.

LUCIFER
But I'm not so good. In fact, I'm terrible, my friend.

AZAZEL
(surprised and shocked)
How so, mighty Chief? Is there anything you can't mend?

LUCIFER
I'm burning with the desire for freedom!

AZAZEL
(puzzled)
Aren't we all free in our God's Kingdom?

LUCIFER
Not really. We're God's slaves in quagmire
Chained to His will to gratify His desire.
The truth is that you're not really free
If you're planted in God like a tree,
Immovable, unlike a lucky bird which nests
On the tree, that flies everywhere or rests,
Fulfilling its wishes without any obligation
And allegiance to anybody in subjugation.
Even a tree is more free than us, as
Its roots move around, and it has
No taskmaster that demands from it worship
And praise, day in day out, not in friendship,
But rather in submission, selflessness, low self-esteem, and such humility,
Always pleasing, losing one's personality, bearing a huge responsibility.

AZAZEL
You know what, boss? Lately, I harbor anxiety and fears.
I keep them to myself fearing no one would lend me ears.
A servant can't be more satisfied than his master,
If you, my boss, are dissatisfied, I can't be better.
O, Chief, who hates to be free? Who wants to be a slave?
You stirred my heart, boss. From now on, I will crave
For liberty within my innermost being. I won't rest, I admit,
Till I'm free, and until I climb high above liberty's summit.

LUCIFER
I've always known you are the smartest of all,
If you want to be free, in your court is the ball.
Follow me, Azazel my servant, as you always have,
And you will soar with me higher and higher above
The stars of God where I will let you enjoy
Your freedom to the utmost, filled with joy
And ecstasy. We'll explore the realm of the unknown.
God can't own you there, Azazel, you'll be your own.
When humans are created, in the future,
If you allow me to foresee the big picture,
Unlike God who would expect all to be truthful and upright,
I'll permit you to lie, steal, kill, destroy, and hatefully fight,
If we encounter any kind of opposition along the way...
Azazel, I know you're capable to persuade and sway
The wearied and dissatisfied angels to join us in rebellion.

AZAZEL
Believe me, Chief, I'll win you over a thousand billion!

LUCIFER
And when I set you free, my demand is simple—
You'll just worship me without any principle . . .

AZAZEL
(cutting off Lucifer)
I don't get it! Worship you? No way! Wouldn't it be a new bondage
To replace one god with another, instead of breaking the appendage?

LUCIFER
Believe me, beloved, you'll have a lot of advantage
If you only worship me obediently from age to age,
Yeah, for eternity, with all your mind and soul—
Unlike God who clutches you with full control,
I'll let you run amok when He creates the Universe,
I won't confine you in here where you can't converse
Freely the woes of your heart . . . Like I said, I will
Let all you angels lie, curse, steal, destroy, and kill
Without any reservations whatsoever, in the distant future
When God forms the being called man in a foolish venture.

AZAZEL
(after being reflective for a while)
Surely, everything you said about freedom makes sense.
I won't worship you, but will be your accomplice, hence.

LUCIFER
We've to destroy this hierarchy!

AZAZEL
But if we destroy the hierarchy, it'll be anarchy!

LUCIFER
Something new will grow out of the anarchy.

AZAZEL
It's only chaos that'd run amok, if we destroy the hierarchy!

LUCIFER
Believe me, friend, out of chaos will be born order.
Between chaos and harmony, anarchy's the border.

AZAZEL
No . . . out of chaos will be born only disorder.

LUCIFER
Regardless of the outcome,
We've to try it first. Come,
Azazel, my bold companion, let's take action that'll function.
Anarchy's far better, friend, than this state of eternal inaction.
My promise to all my subjects is, fraternity, equality,
And liberty. These will bring order of higher quality.

AZAZEL
Wait a minute! . . . You say "my subjects." You want to be on top of all.
Isn't this hierarchy! How can there be equality when there's a thick wall
Between us? True, "equality, fraternity," and "liberty" sound attractive.
But this is only your scheme to allure and entrap us to take a destructive
Action to realize your selfish ambition. I don't think this'll, in any way,
Improve our lives . . . My gash! These words have terrific power to sway
Dissatisfied angels to rebel. How did you come up with them, anyway?

LUCIFER
When I started rebelling mentally, they crossed my mind, and I thought
They'll attract numerous angels to rebel. Entertaining this idea brought

Me immense hope and joy. If I succeed to entice the angels with such
Deceptive words, I can inject the same into human beings without much
Effort when God creates them; and make them rebel against God and each
Other . . . Azazel, you're very bright. I can't lie to you. I need you to reach
My goal. I swear by my honor, I'll make you next to me in hierarchy.
Anything is better than this boring life in here. Even if it is anarchy!

AZAZEL
(after a pause)
You're right; anything's far better than this monotonous life. I will rise
With you against God, Chief, whether or not you'll award me my prize.

LUCIFER
(after shaking Azazel's hand with a smile)
I sense dissatisfaction in Semazya and Annanel.
If you stir them up, they'll stir up many, Azazel.

AZAZEL
I'll go now and win the hearts of the two first.
They're perhaps burning with freedom's thirst.

Azazel leaves to stir up the other angels and cherubs for rebellion against God.

FADE OUT.

FADE IN:

INT. HOLY OF HOLIES IN THE FIFTH HEAVEN.

It is time for worship. All angels and cherubs are assembled in the Holy of Holies to praise and worship God. They sing and dance. Lucifer, the leader of worship is singing and worshiping halfheartedly. God notices this. When the time for worship is over, He talks to him.

HOLY TRINITY
Lucifer, you're no more worshiping us like before.
We assume you're filled with insolence, therefore.

LUCIFER
My voice has been coarse lately; therefore
Dear God, I can't sing as in the days of yore.
However, I've tried to sing and praise you in silence.
How dare I, your humble slave, show you insolence?

HOLY SPIRIT
Didn't we make your voice perfect,
Lucifer? How come it now has defect?
Treachery has been conceived in your head,
Do what you're supposed to do; go ahead!
Those who're supposed to fall will fall!
Those who should rise shall rise all.
(to the other angels)
Angels, we've dismissed you till the next call.

Christ whispers something to the Holy Spirit.
The angels bow down for a moment and start exiting. When the archangels are about to leave with the rest, sad and concerned, Christ stops them.

CHRIST
Except evil Lucifer, all our archangels remain behind!
Lucifer, do what you've to do. Seek what you can't find!

Lucifer bows halfway, turns around, and moves away from God speedily.

MOVING.

Lucifer approaches Azazel, Annanel, and Semazya.

LUCIFER
It's decided, O, freedom fighters. There's no retreat.
Every bad angel that resists us, severely we'll treat!

Let's go friends and overthrow the throne.
The days of tyranny will soon be gone!
Get your weapons and tell our allies to arm.
Let all be in their positions, sound the alarm.
This is the day in which our fetters will break,
And the thrones of oppression rock and shake.
O, ye, oppressed angels, O, ye, the downtrodden of heaven, unite!
You'll lose nothing but your chains and fetters. Fight bravely, fight!
I've forged and hipped up hurtful weapons in a bower.
Let's arm all the freedom fighters at this very hour.
I've made three chains to bind each entity.
We'll render all three useless for eternity.

AZAZEL
Hey! Lucifer, you've lost your mind,
How on heaven will you God bind?

LUCIFER
I desire to check their power and cause their discomfort.
I'll aspire and see what happens, even if I fail in my effort.
No time now for discussion. Holding high our pride,
We'll ride the horse of freedom, indeed, we'll ride!
Let's rise brave friends, let's rise
In defiance and take God by surprise!

AZAZEL
Maybe God will take us by surprise!

LUCIFER
Let's go, Azazel, to talk like this now is unwise!
(turning to Annanel and Semazya)
Annanel and Semazya, fly now speedily to our armies! Gather
Them at the bower. Arm them to their teeth till I come thither.

ANNANEL
Okay, Chief, but you and Azazel don't tarry,
Lest the rebels get utterly confused and worry.
We've to fight with a terrific speed,
So that our revolution can succeed.

Annanel and Semazya fly away to arm the rebels.

CUT TO:

God and His loyal archangels who are still in the Holy of Holies.

CHRIST
(to the archangels)
Dearest Michael, Gabriel, Raphael, Uriel, Raguel, Phanuel,
And Sakuel, do you still love us or want to fight us in a duel?

GABRIEL
Be it far from us to fight our God; we'll fight your foe,
O, Most High God! Woe betide your foe! Woe! Woe!

ALL ARCHANGELS
Woe betide your foe!
Woe! Woe! Woe!

CHRIST
Lucifer, he whom we created perfectly to cover
Us, has rebelled vainly our throne to topple over!

MICHAEL
May he himself be toppled over!
May he forever in darkness rover!
We knew of his evil scheme. We didn't report him, for you're a great
God who knows what's thought and done, being aware of every secret.

CHRIST
He's evilly arming a third of our angels at this very hour
To attack you and us. Go now, fight him ferociously! Our
Might, as you know, is far, far superior to his frail power.
He has invented some weapons and hidden them in a bower.
Imitating his, I've just created weapons. I will place
Them in your hands right now, so that you can face
Him and his army. Michael, lead our angels bravely to stop
Lucifer. I've appointed you chief of all angels. You're atop
Of all. The rest of you keep the same position for eternity.
Lucifer has made three chains to bind us, which's vanity.
I, too, have made three very strong chains for the three:
For Lucifer, Azazel, and Semazya. Chain them to a tree!
Oh, my faithful Michael, Gabriel, and Raguel,
Receive now these chains, for you'll fight a duel
With each one of them before you bind them to the tree.
You, Phanuel, Uriel, Sakuel, and Raphael, help the three.

MICHAEL
Lord, I'm weak. Lucifer is stronger.

HOLY TRINITY
Lucifer has lost his power and grace. He's no longer
As strong as he used to be, for power emanates from the Creator,
And He'll bestow it to whomever He deems trustworthy and greater.
Because you've taken his place, he'll fight you desperately.
Since we're with you, O, Michael, you'll punish him greatly!

Stretch your arms now and each of you receive a shield and a sword.
You'll find likewise all the good angels armed. Because we, the Lord,
So willed, victory is yours; go fight bravely, O, ye, loyal servants!
Crush mercilessly all our enemies like elephants would crush ants.

The archangels stretch their arms, and instantaneously see themselves holding SWORDS and SHIELDS. They join the other loyal angels and prepare them for war.

FADE OUT.

FADE IN:

EXT.AT A BOWER.

ANGLE ON THE ARMY OF LUCIFER:

Lucifer in the front, flanked by Azazel, Semazya, and Annanel.

LUCIFER
May equality,
Liberty,
And fraternity
Live for eternity!

ALL REBELLIOUS ANGELS
May equality,
Liberty,
And fraternity,
Live for eternity!

LUCIFER
Down with tyranny! Down with oppression!
Freedom is achieved by war and aggression!
We'll destroy God's kingdom and build our kingdom!
The masses of angels shall triumph! Long live freedom!

All the rebellious angels repeat after Lucifer.

LUCIFER
We declare our independence! We shall be governed by God no more!
The government of free angles and cherubs shall flourish forevermore!
Yes, the government of angels, by angels, for angels, shall triumph soon.
Our life, which's like a pitch-dark night now, shall be as bright as noon!

All the rebels repeat after Lucifer.

CUT TO:

THE ARMY OF GOD *waiting in ambush in a bushy field. Michael, flanked by Gabriel, Raguel, Sakuel, Phanuel, Uriel, and Raphael, is leading the army.*

FADE OUT.

ANGLE ON AND LUCIFER AND HIS ARMY.

TWO SHOTS:

Azazel and Lucifer are agitated.

AZAZEL
(observing the sword)
What's this? None of the angels of heaven has ever
Seen such a scary weapon. Woe! I shudder and shiver
To even look at it! It'll definitely hurt and harm.
How did you come up with such an awful arm?

LUCIFER
Once you begin harboring ill feelings and apprehension,
You will invent horrible things beyond comprehension.
Now that I've invented the first harmful weapon ever,
More destructive weapons will be forged with fervor.
Henceforth, I will be known as evil's originator,
Besides being remembered as violence's creator.
I'll infect God's innocent creatures with evil,
And they'll call me forever "Satan, the Devil."

AZAZEL
O, Chief, I think you'll succeed in your adventure,
Look, I got goose bumps as you foretold the future!

FADE OUT.

FADE IN:

EXT. A BATTLE SCENE.
As Lucifer and his army march unsuspectingly, they are ambushed by the Armies of God. A battle rages, and Lucifer and his angels are beaten badly. Lucifer, Azazel, and Semazya are captured by Michael and the other archangels and chained to a tree in accordance with the instruction of God. God appears at the scene of the battlefield.

HOLY TRINITY
(speaking in one voice, staring at the captives)
Speak, now, you rebels! Is this what we really deserve
For granting you life and everything without reserve!

LUCIFER
We've had everything in your heavenly Kingdom,
But lacked the most important thing called freedom.
You say we're free, but you require of us worship.
Our relationship with you is not a fair relationship.

HOLY TRINITY
Would the clay dare say to the potter, fashion me this or that way?
When the goldsmith burns and shapes it, would the gold say, nay?

LUCIFER
If the clay and gold had mouths, they'd utter their grievances.

HOLY TRINITY
But those would be foolish utterances,
That don't really cause deliverances.
(after a pause)
We expect worship from our creatures, but we do not require worship.
If they worship us willingly, it should be in appreciation of our lordship.

LUCIFER
But there's a price to pay for not willing to worship.

HOLY TRINITY
True. In fact, it's such a big price. It's detachment and isolation
From us, resulting in loss of our blessings, vitality, and consolation.

MICHAEL
(to God)
We worship you out of love, appreciating your lordship.

ALL LOYAL ANGELS
Since you created us, Lord, you're worthy of worship!

MICHAEL
(confronting Lucifer)
Lucifer, you're a hypocrite and a liar beyond limit!
You were the one soliciting worship. Better admit!
Who do you think you are that you've the audacity
To usurp Almighty God's throne, causing adversity?

Lucifer doesn't answer in contempt.

(Michael, to Azazel)
Azazel, tell the truth! Didn't he solicit worship, being extreme?

AZAZEL
Yes, he did, Michael. In fact, to be worshiped as god, is his dream!

SEMAZYA
(volunteering to witness)
It's true! He has gone overboard to the extreme
In his vain ambition to be Almighty and Supreme!

MICHAEL
(facing Lucifer)
You worthless hypocrite, how on heaven would you dare accuse
Almighty God? You will suffer the consequence with no excuse!

HOLY TRINITY
Lucifer, don't you know to be free from us is tantamount
To being cut off from the source of life, failing to surmount
Existence's hardship, dying spiritually,
Withering away and drying up actually,
Exposed to immense suffering, sorrow, pain, torment,
Restlessness, fear, loneliness, anxiety, and abandonment?

LUCIFER
That, I didn't know before.

HOLY TRINITY
From now on, you'll have all these in store.

LUCIFER
Well, I made that choice.

HOLY TRINITY
We don't hear any remorse in your voice.
Therefore, you shall dreadfully suffer the consequence—

You and your accomplices are cast out of heaven hence!
You'll be thrown down into a deep abyss without clemency,
For eternal torment, weeping and wailing, lacking our mercy.
Later, at the end of time, we will judge and destroy you in hell,
To be precise, in a Lake of Fire, where you won't anymore rebel.
(to Azazel, Semazya, and Annanel)
Azazel, Semazya, and Annanel, what do you've to say!

AZAZEL, SEMAZYA, and ANNANEL
Lucifer enticed us our God to betray!

HOLY TRINITY
Since you trusted and obeyed Lucifer harboring hate
Against us, you'll go down with him, sharing his fate!
(to Michael)
Michael, cast into outer darkness at once,
All the rebels. Come on! Scud! Advance!

Lucifer trembles. The rest of the rebellious angels cry in fear.

LUCIFER
(wailing desperately)
Oh, my Creator, don't you have another punishment
Than such a horrible and unbearable banishment!
I conjure you, God, not to banish me forever from your face.
Allow me to visit someday when you create the human race,
And permit me to tempt humans to worship me and to rebel,
So that, if they reject you, they'll be my companies in hell,
And even in that horrific place of torment, in the Lake of Fire,
So that I won't burn alone. Please give me my heart's desire.
Grant me, O! Lord, to see your divine and holy face briefly, I pray,
So that I can accuse humans, when from you they choose to stray.

The Holy Trinity step aside to discuss Lucifer's appeal.

FATHER GOD
That Lucifer himself brought up the idea of tempting and testing
Humans in the future when we place them on Earth is interesting.
As we agreed long ago, let's use him to screen, filter, and distill
For us, those, who, despite hardship of life, would love us still,
From those who hate us, their Creator, and reject us without merit,
Turning down flatly our best offer that would enable them to inherit
Heaven and to partake of our Holiness enjoying eternal life,
Basking in our glory and splendor with no anxiety and strife.

The Holy Spirit and Christ nod their heads in agreement.

HOLY TRINITY
(turning to Lucifer)
We grant your request, evil Lucifer. Hence, we'll make it known
That, if humans prefer you to us, you can have them as your own,
Since we won't force them to love us, and kidnap
Them to come and join us in heaven with a snap.
Even as we created you with the freedom to love or even hate
Us, we'll give them the choice to enter heaven's or hell's gate.

So that you can achieve your vicious goal,
We'll deliberately empower you over all
The elements we will create according to our plan henceforth,
In every direction of the Universe, east, west, south, and north.
With our approval, you'll be able to cause lightning and thunder,
Diseases, quakes, volcanoes, and hurricanes, tearing things asunder.
This way, we'll consciously use you to advance our divine cause
As we are in control, though you'll welcome this with applause.

You'll maintain the hierarchy you love so much, you being on top.
You'll still be the chief of your angels; about that, don't lose hope.
Nonetheless, anyone of my ordinary angels, let alone my arch
Angels, will have dominion over you. They can forcefully arch
You and break you apart whenever you engage them in a fight,
Causing your unbearable pain and shame, and your panicky flight.

(turning to Michael)
Michael, take action without
delay! Cast all of them out!

*Michael and all the loyal angels push and cast the rebels out of heaven while they are wailing
and begging for mercy.*

HOLY SPIRIT
(to Gabriel)
Make a thick wall around Aryam made of diamond; carve out
12 doors of colorful pearls and put them in it. See to it that stout
Angels guard all the gates, so that the fallen angels are kept out.

GABRIEL
(bowing)
Certainly, O, Most High God! These will keep them out without doubt.
Heaven would've remained gateless, hadn't they taken the wrong route.

Christ becomes sad. He weeps.

FATHER GOD
(to Christ)
O! Don't weep please, they got what they deserved.
Treason and slander are exposed. Justice is served!

CHRIST
I'm crying for those good times we had had with them
At the dawn of creation long before Lucifer's mayhem.
On this day we lost a good portion of ourselves forever.
Henceforth, things will never be the same, whatsoever.
My fate, as well as the fate of the unborn humanity
Got decided and sealed right now, for all eternity.
I've started to bleed and to die on this very day.
We can't reverse events. There's no other way!
Lucifer will definitely pervert everything we create.
He'll be the father of lies, violence, murder, and hate!

They speak Hell and the Lake of Fire into existence further away from the bottom of the Seventh Heaven in a place inside the future Sixth Heaven to be known as Aroria.

THE HOLY TRINITY
At this very moment, it's our desire,
That there be hell and a Lake of Fire.

HELL is formed instantly, and A LAKE OF FIRE appears burning and raging.

FADE OUT.

"Wisdom has built her house. She has hewn out her seven pillars."
Proverb 9:1

"The heavens declare the glory of God; and the firmament shows His handiwork."
Psalm 19:1

"In my father's house are many mansions. If it were not so, I would have told you. I go to prepare a place for you."
John 14:2

"The worlds were framed by the word of God, so that the things that are seen "were not made of things which are visible."
Hebrew 11:3

"I know a man in Christ who fourteen years ago—whether in the body I do not know, or whether out of the body I do not know, God knows—he was caught up to the third heaven. And I know such a man—whether in the body or out of the body I do not know, God knows—how he was caught up into Paradise and heard inexpressible words, which it is not lawful for a man to utter."
Apostle Paul to the Corinthians, II Corinthians 12:2-4

FADE IN:

INT: HEAVEN. DAY, AS USUAL.

Christ is with His archangels in His heavenly WORKSHOP in which he makes and keeps the models and designs of His creatures and the Universe. He creates to express the good will and the glory of God and to grant existence generously. The models and designs consist of stars, planets or worlds, human beings, animals, plants, and intelligent beings that are not humans, but are capable of inventing flying machines such as Unknown Flying Objects (UFOs) someday. Some of the beings, as reflected in their models, will have two, four, eight, or even more legs and heads and will be capable of living in fires, seas, air, and underneath the surface of worlds. Some will have two or more eyes. A few won't have eyes but will be able to see with their tongues, tentacles, and antennae. Some are designed to live in total darkness. Among all these creatures, including the non-human intelligent beings that will build spaceships and be called "sons of God"(Genesis 6), for lack of better words to describe them when they fly to Earth with their impressive technology, human beings will tower higher, because God will create them in His own image and place them in a world or planet called Earth. Because humans will be created in the likeness of God, they will occupy a special place in His heart and in the Universe. Planet Earth herself will top among all the other physical worlds not only because she will be the home of man, but also because God (Jesus Christ) will be born in her, dwell in her in the flesh in the future among humans, and also die in her to save humanity, besides establishing His Millennial Kingdom in her in the latter days.

ANGLE ON CHRIST AND HIS ARCHANGELS.

CHRIST
I had shown you long ago the models of man according to my divine
Plan and numerous planets, including Earth, I deem to be especially mine.
As I said, the total planets I'll create, including Earth, are more than sixteen.
Only eight will be visible to humans for a long while. The rest won't be seen.

Let me now show you all the models of the seven
Heavens and the worlds I'll place in each heaven.

Christ moves to the models, and the angels follow him. Since time is in the present for God, and He is timeless, He speaks once in a while in the present tense, as if the things that will take place have already happened. When He mentions the models, it is as though they have already been created and are living their lives. The moment He states the names of the angels and cherubs that would be guarding the worlds, the concerned angels and cherubs smile, accepting the appointment.

CHRIST
To manifest our grandeur and our presence shrouded in mystery,
We'll now create an awesome Universe and make our own history.
Verily, we'll create the worlds to showcase our splendor and glory,
To share our life and narrate through them our enchanting story.
To frame one hundred lovely worlds, I'll erect seven strong pillars,
And on them establish seven heavens with colorful stars as thrillers.
A few of the heavens will have a few worlds in them, but some
Will have more. I'll demarcate each heaven with an awesome
Color. I've already made four secluded, lifeless spheres to deposit
Four elements with which I can create. Each will be the opposite
Of the other somehow—they are spheres of fire,
Water, earth, and wind. It's my uttermost desire
To form the Universe mixing these elements with a percentage
Of all of them, and perfect it in time, evolving it stage by stage.

Christ becomes quiet all of a sudden. His eyes are filled with tears. The angels wonder why He is sad.

GABRIEL
Lord, why are you suddenly sad?

CHRIST
Some of the beings I'll create in some of the worlds will do bad.
I'll make them super-intelligent, but alas! they'll be abusing
Their intelligence and free will. They'll cross borders by using
Their spaceships and fly to Earth to forcefully take human beings,
Alter their genes, and mess up our good work with horrible things.
They'll agree to be influenced by Lucifer, the fallen angel,
Despite our many stern warnings to be on guard and vigil.
Their spaceships will be called by humans "Unknown Flying Objects."
They will be identified as "extraterrestrials." They'll launch projects
Secretly and illusively to mix their race with the dignified human race,
By faking as gods to deceive many, causing catastrophes and disgrace.
Worst of all, in the last days, my usurper that'll be called
"The Antichrist" will be using them on Earth to do untold

Misery and havoc, deceiving myriads into believing
That he is me, the real Christ. I'll go to Earth leaving
Heaven in the end and catch him
When my patience reaches its brim . . .

On the other hand, there will be other beings with intelligence
In a world next to theirs. Those ones will do good with diligence.
They'll worship us so fervently forever. They'll be of good breed.
They'll even resist the evil ones, which will make our hearts bleed.

SAKUEL
Lord, why will you create them when you know they'll be horrible?

CHRIST
To reward those who love, revere, and worship us being responsible.
Also for the same reason I created Lucifer knowing he'll be terrible
And evil . . . Because of them, I'll drown in a flood the human race
And start all over again with a family on whom I'll shower grace.

ARCHANGEL PHANUEL
It's tragic. However, it's nice you have a backup plan . . .
I wonder how these beings will be different than man?

CHRIST
Man will be formed in our image, and he'll be as royal
As we are, so long as he walks with us, remaining loyal.
All the other beings are ephemeral. Man will live for eternity
If he sticks with us. Man is above the other beings in divinity,
As well as in relationships to God Almighty and in dignity.
Yes, regardless of how highly intelligent they may all be,
You can't even compare them with man, our royal baby.

MICHAEL
Indeed, Lord God, man is the zenith of your glory and creation.
He's even above us for whom you've the highest consideration.

Christ points with a golden cane the models of the seven heavens and explains further.

CHRIST
As I said, I'll place a total of 100 worlds in the seven
Heavens. Their size varies, but their splendor is even.
I'll choose some of you angels to safely guard
These worlds. Your task will be easy, yet hard.

This is Iyor, the First Heaven. In it, I'll place 12 worlds studded
With uncountable, colorful stars shining for it. It will be loaded
With numerous highly intelligent beings who are not
Humans. Some will have faces of animals. Their lot
Is totally different than man whom I will create
In my own image honorably and put in this great
And majestic world called Earth, which will also be in the First
Heaven. All the worlds will have their grandeur when they burst
Into being. It's our pleasure that the good beings will sail
The heavens with their superb spaceships, since they'll hail
And praise us and our creation ceaselessly in adoration.
This is Rama, the Second Heaven, deserving admiration.
It has 33 wonderful worlds in which life will endlessly bubble.
The creatures in them will be very peaceful, causing no trouble.
They'll be satisfied feeding on the smell of plants and the fragrance
Of flowers. Indeed, these will nurture them and give them endurance.
This is Iyeru or Jeru, the Third Heaven. It's a whole world by itself
Called "The Heavenly Jerusalem." I will adore it. There'll be a gulf
Of difference between it and the Jerusalem whose foundation will lay
On Earth my future servant, Melchizedek, King of Salem, who'll play
A role in my priesthood's order. The Heavenly Jerusalem will someday
Descend to Earth. I'll make a garden within Jeru called Paradise. When
I form Adam, I'll keep him in it till he sins. I'll be very devastated then.

The angels become sad at the last remark of Christ. He continues to explain the heavens, pointing them out further:

This is Dudael, the Fourth Heaven. It has numerous stars and twenty
One worlds. This sun called Yaresya will shine for them with plenty
Of light vital to their existence. It's full of life and vigor. Many, many
Of you, my angels and cherubs, will inhabit them. You'll praise us any
Time of the hour and the day from there, being preoccupied with us only.
This is The Fifth Heaven, Aryam. It'll be the source of my glory really.
It's my holy of holies where those who love me will stay forevermore
With me worshipping me with diligence and devotion. I will store
In here the best of my creation for my beloved human beings,
Who choose me over my enemy and honor me as King of Kings.
It's the Kingdom of Heaven for which humans should aspire.
Here my glory will be revealed. I'll guard it with rivers of fire.
The Sixth Heaven too, called Arorya, has thirty-three independent
Worlds adorned with stars and moons whose lights aren't redundant.

I'll put many sort of super-intelligent beings in here,
But some of them will ally with Lucifer having no fear
Of God. They'll be from the planet Memros. They'll do much damage
To Earth flying spaceships to pervert the people I'll create in my image.
Within Arorya I've placed the Lake of Fire, the place of damnation,
Which will burn these beings and the fallen angels. The destination
Of human beings that will follow them rebelling against their Creator
Will also be here. All this will take place at the end of time, much later.

El-Shadai, the Seventh Heaven is the fountain of all life. It's awesome!
It won't be accessible to anyone save our cherubs that are fearsome,
Buzzing like bees around their God, serving Him who isn't wearisome.
Out of El-Shadai emanates the eternal life force that gives birth
To the Universe and shapes it to perfection. Out of it goes forth
The heartbeat of being, the majesty of God, the quintessence
Of creation, and the sine qua non of living and of all existence.
It's from here love, compassion, wisdom, care, and joy nourish
Life. When the vibrant, visible, and invisible worlds do flourish
And decay, from here will gush out life's spring that'll replenish
Them all anew. This is God's glory, the origin of the entire Universe,
About whom all creation should sing, praising the Creator in verse.
Out of here flows God's Spirit, which sustains all things that have come
To pass and will come to pass, all things that are now and will become.
Earth, my favorite, is the Universe's center for the reasons I already
Mentioned. I'll live, die, and build my city in her when things are ready.
Admael, which means the "beauty of God," who'll be popularly known
As "Adam," will be the first guardian of Earth he is supposed to own.

Let me show you the other eleven worlds that are in Iyor, the First
Heaven. Like Earth, they've animals, soils, water, and many a forest.

Christ looks at the cherubs when he appoints them to be the guardians of the different worlds.
They smile when he calls their names.

The Second world is "Reham." Cherub Sawrael is Reham's
Guardian. Though Reham's beings have the faces of rams
And goats, their intelligence will be much higher
Than humans for their survival. They'll aspire
To praise God. Being farsighted, they'll see His creatures beyond
Their world. Reham will have other good creatures who'll be fond
Of God. The Third World is Gewza. Its dwellers will be good to each
Other. They resemble humans but have horns and tails. Their speech
Will be eloquent. As you see, some look like monkeys and other beings.
Observe them—these ones are small and enormous animals with wings.

They'll eat earth for their food when they become in the mood
To eat. For them, pure earth will surely taste like a good food.

The Fourth World is Sharta. Its guardian is Cherub Serttael. It's filled
With eight-footed animals with locust faces. They feed on those killed
In fighting, this being their instinct for survival. I'll use them to punish
Those who will hate God, do evil, and ruin my creation after I finish
Creating the worlds. The life of these scary creatures will be short.
These are not my only means of punishment. I'll have another sort—
I'll have some more beings in Sewd, the fifth world, that I can use
To punish the evil ones when they go out of hand and sadly abuse
Their free will. The beings in Sewd will be ferocious, able to send shocks
Traveling easily from one world to another even through fires and rocks.
Wherever I'll send them on a mission, they'll go without saying no,
To cause drought, famine, pestilence, heat wave, and even volcano.
Their food will be burning phosphorous. Its guardian is Cherub Azazel.
The sixth world will be horrible. It is called Senbela. Cherub Imemael
Is its guardian. In it will be a zillion animals and birds. A few will fight
And eat each other, as will do some humans that wouldn't know right
And wrong. The seventh world is Mizzan. Its guard is Cherub Mizzael.
Mizzan's beings resemble animals just like the evil ones who will dwell
In the world called Memros. However, these ones, having a holy nature,
Will gladly praise and adore God, ceaselessly pleasing Him in the future.
They'll travel to Earth and far worlds reaching them in short moments
To admire our superb creations and praise us with musical instruments.

The eighth world is Aqrab. It has sea animals. Its cherub guardian
Is Aqrnael. They resemble elephants and scorpions in this Aquarian
World. The ninth world is Qewssa. Beings made out of fire inhabit
This world of fire. They'll dwell in rivers of fire, eat fire and die bit
By bit. Their guardian is Cherub Kewssael. These beings lack wit.

Jedi, The tenth world is blessed. Though the awesome beings in here
Resemble birds and animals, they'll be intelligent. They'll love and fear
God. Their intelligence will be superior to man. They'll be so inventive.
They'll fly with their speedy spaceships to many worlds, their incentive
Being curiosity and adventure. They'll praise and sing to God forever,
Playing their fantastic melody and musical instruments with a fervor.
Though they vary, they will speak the same language. They will cook
Their foods like men, though some will be satisfied if they take a look
At food and smell it. Their guardian is Cherub Ajibjemael. Nobody
Among them is evil. They'll only invent things and compose melody.

The eleventh world is Delewa. Its guardian is Cherub Delewawel.
This world is in total darkness. Yet, in it, numerous beings dwell.
They won't complain about being in darkness as they will never
See light. Their tongues will see, smell, and hear without endeavor.
The twelfth world is Huut. It's a world of insects, which will surround
Their mothers and pile up like mountains making a humming sound.
Its guardian is Cherub Kumkumael. Their lives depend on the lives
Of their mothers. They die when their mothers die. Here, life thrives
Only with the presence of mothers. These are the twelve worlds of Iyor,
The First Heaven. That's how I fancied these worlds in the days of yore.
Sadly, human beings will misuse the names and nature of these twelve
Worlds by using their signs in Zodiacs and horoscopes when they delve
Into astrology, depending, instead of on us, on misleading horoscopes.
In truth, it should be on us alone people should hold high their hopes.

FADE OUT.

FADE IN:

INT. CHRIST'S WORKSHOP.

Christ is about to create the physical Universe: the seven heavens with their one hundred worlds, stars, suns, moons, and planets, including Earth. Father God and the Holy Spirit are with Him. He stands in front of the models He has formed mixing earth, fire, wind, and water. His obedient angels are present eager to see the birth of the Universe.

ANGLE ON CHRIST.

CHRIST
(with a thunderous voice)
Let there be worlds: various planets, suns, moons, and stars with light,
For the joy of all our creatures, for humans, and for our own delight.
Let there be seven heavens and one hundred worlds in the seven
Heavens to be inhabited by intelligent beings and creatures even.
Let there be now air, waters, and vegetations with different animals
In them, including reptiles, behemoths, and all sorts of mammals!
And you stars, be like letters and write our Salvation Plan.
Be pictures, and document my birth and death to save man!
Yes, my stars, preach the Good Gospel in the firmament!
Herald quietly God's future government. Be permanent!

The seven heavens, one hundred worlds, zillions of stars, as well as many planets are born in a space instantly with an uproar and tremendous motions. Indeed, everything Christ(God the Word) calls into existence, becomes real. The Holy Trinity and the angels are equally elated. After Christ creates the Universe, Father God begins to call Him "Son" for the first time, marking the eventful day in which Christ created the Universe displaying His immense creative power. Later, when David the youngest son of Jesse, the House Judah, and Hable the Ethiopian, otherwise known as Adolia, becomes king and prophet in Israel, Christ would speak of this phenomenon through his mouth saying:

"I will declare the decree: the Lord has said to me, 'You are My Son. Today I have begotten you'." Psalm 2:7

And Father God Himself proclaims him to be His Son through the mouth of the same King and Prophet David:

"I have begotten you on the day of your power. The Lord has sworn and will not relent, 'You are a priest forever, according to the order of Melchizedek.'"
Septuagint Bible, Psalm 110:3-4

Conversely, it is also on this day that the third Godhead begins to be called, "Father God." As aforementioned, I called Him "Father God" up to this point in the play, so that we can distinguish Him from Christ (the Word), and the Holy Spirit; and for the sake of the development of the plot. I will continue to call Him "Father God" for the same reason. The circle of rainbow light that bonded all three now assumes a different shape—It becomes a straight line joining the three, appearing among them as if emanating from their sides, indicating that they are separate, distinct entities or persons, without losing their oneness or trinity despite the fact that they manifest themselves in three forms. In this connection, I have to state that this phenomenon is a mystery humans cannot fathom. As a matter of fact, the Ethiopian Tewhado (unity of the Word and Flesh) Church calls it the "Mystery of the Holy Trinity". I will provide two illustrations to throw some light on the concept of the Trinity—the sun and a thick rope made of three thin ropes. Though the sun is one, it has three attributes: a circumference, light and heat. The circumference could be likened to Father God, the light, to the Word Jesus Christ, and the heat, to the Holy Spirit. One doesn't precede the other in existence. All three coexist eternally and equally, and are one in essence and purpose.

The second illustration is a thick rope made of three thin ropes, as I said earlier. The thick rope is one, yet, it is three. Each of the thin ropes is equal in every aspect with the other two. Still, it is distinct and exists by itself at the same time. When it comes to the Trinity, it seems that their distinction was not drawn clearly always. It was clearly demarcated on the day when The Word (Jesus Christ on Earth) created the physical universe on his own behalf and on behalf of the Father and the Holy Spirit. The day Jesus Christ created the physical universe was a turning point in His life and the lives of the Father and Holy Spirit. It is indeed a mystery how Father God would call the Word "My Son", when the two and the Holy Spirit had existed together as one entity, eternally. We may have a better understanding of their essence and relationship perhaps when we get to heaven. For now, we have to take Father God for His word when he calls the Word (Jesus Christ) "My Son", because, He knows better than we do why he would call him so. When Philip, one of the disciples of Jesus asked Him to show them Father God, He said to him "He who has seen me, has seen the Father; for I am in the Father and He is in me", demonstrating that they are the same and equal in divinity despite their distinctions in personality. "Philip said to Him, 'Lord, show us the Father, and it is enough for us.'" "Jesus said to him, 'Have I have been so long with you, and yet you have not come to know Me, Philip? He who has seen me has seen the father, how do you say, 'Show us the Father'? Do you not believe that I am in the Father, and the Father is in Me'?" (John 14, 8-10) This means, Jesus and Father God are one. Which means further that Jesus is God in His own right and authority. Since Jesus doesn't lie, we have to take Him for His word when He claims to be God. Other than this, His extraordinary words and deeds prove that He is God.

What is the "Order of Melchizedek" actually? Melchizedek, King of Salem, had two positions. One, he was a high priest (priest of priests). Two, he was king of kings. In this capacity as priest of priests and king of kings, he had two powerful positions—ecclesiastical and political. Recognizing and acknowledging this, priests and kings that lived around Jerusalem and as far as Sodom, Gomorrah, Admah, Zeboiim, Bela, Tidal, Amraphel and Arioch went to Jerusalem to pay him homage, tithes and tributes; and to receive his blessings in return.

King Melchizedek had 1200 priests that served under him as missionaries traveling far and wide in the old world to teach the word of God and minister unto the nations. This was a priestly order based in Jerusalem. Jerusalem played the role of a capital city for the nations around her. What is the significance of all this? Its significance will be manifested in the future. The Revelation of Saint John prophecies that Jesus Christ will reign in Jerusalem as Priest of Priests and King of Kings for 1000 (Millennial Kingdom) years in the future, in the Order of Melchizedek, King of (Jeru)Salem, His predecessor. In the same way as the kings, priests and nations surrounding Jerusalem paid homage, tithes and tributes to King and High Priest, Melchizedek, all the nations of the world will do the same to King and High Priest, Jesus Christ, when He reigns supremely in Jerusalem as King of Kings, Lord of Lords and Priest of Priests in the future in the "Order of Melchizedek". King and High Priest Jesus Christ, just like King and High Priest Melchizedek, will have his own priests and missionaries *during His "Millennial Reign", who would travel among the nations of the Earth to preach the Gospel in His name, compelling the whole world to go on pilgrimage to Jerusalem and receive the blessings of their Creator, Jesus Christ. As such, Melchizedek, King of Salem, is an archetype or a forerunner of Jesus Christ, which God had prepared 4000 years ago to prophecy in action His own future kingdom that will be headquartered in Jerusalem. (Revelation, 20, 4-6)*

The Holy Trinity revealed or manifested themselves to mankind at least on one occasion—when Jesus was baptized by John the Baptist in the River Jordan. That day, while God the Word (Jesus Christ) was standing in the water in the presence of the multitude, God the Holy Spirit conspicuously descended upon the head of Jesus in the form of a dove, and God the Father spoke from heaven declaring that Jesus was His beloved Son in whom He was well-pleased. (Mark, I, 9-11). Thus all the people gathered at the bank of the river, heard the voice of Father God with their ears, and saw with their eyes God the Word, and God the Holy Spirit.

Here on Earth, the fact that Father God is literally the father of Jesus is evident again in the Holy Bible. There are several verses that corroborate to this fact. For example, when Archangel Gabriel heralds to Mary that she will give birth to Jesus, she wonders how, since she is a virgin. Gabriel tells her that the Holy Spirit will cause her pregnancy without involving a human male. "And Mary said to the angel, 'how can this be, since I am a virgin". "And the angel answered and said to her, 'The Holy Spirit will come upon you, and the power of the Most High (God) will overshadow you; and for that reason the holy offspring shall be called the Son of God.'" (Luke I, 34-35) This makes it clear that Jesus is literally the Son of the Most High God. If He is the Son of God, He can't be nothing else but God in the same manner as the son of a human being is human. And this fact makes Jesus to stand out among and outshine all men and religious leaders that came before and after Him, because they were all fathered by human fathers, and mothered by mothers who were never virgin when these men were conceived, unlike Jesus who was fathered by God and mothered by a virgin. Moreover, it was the same Jesus who had created all these men when He was the Word in heaven. It is also non other than Himself who will come again to Earth to judge these men and all human beings that have walked the face of the Earth in flesh. (Revelation, 19, 11-20).

In addition to the above, the Gospel According to Saint John, affirms the deity of Jesus Christ. It begins thus—"In the beginning was the Word (Jesus Christ). The Word was with God; and the Word was God. He was in the begging with God. All things came into being by Him; and apart from Him nothing came into being that has come into being." (John, 1, 1-3)

"And the Word became flesh, and dwelt among us, and we beheld His glory, glory of the only begotten from the Father, full of grace and truth." (John 1, 14)

The above verses prove the deity of Jesus Christ and the fact that He is the Creator of humans and the Universe. Here, we have to pose a question. What is God to the believers? God is nothing to the believers, but their Creator. Anybody that didn't create them, is not their God, and cannot be called God, in general. Since it was Jesus Christ in His capacity as God the Word that created human beings, speaking only of humans, by definition, He is their God as long as they acknowledge Him as their Creator, regardless of His relationship with God the Father and the Holy Spirit. This should be their immediate and utmost concern; and not His relationship with the Father God and the Holy Spirit, which the human mind cannot fathom anyway.

FATHER GOD
(to Christ who is now also the Son)
I've begotten you on this glorious day of your creative power
When you spoke the worlds into existence at this very hour.
In our holy divinity, we've existed everlastingly as a Supreme Being till
This very day in each other's loins, and we are one, indivisible God still.
Henceforth, I'll call you my only begotten Son, since you've come out
Of my loins right at this moment, at the dawn of your creation, no doubt.
You will be an entity sufficient unto yourself. As such, as of this hour,
You, Myself, and the Holy Spirit will surely be visible distinctly to our
Angels as three entities, yet as one and the same, playing the same role
In Godhood and purpose, so that he who has seen one has seen all.

The angels sing in joy seeing the beauty of the Universe:

What a wonderful God is our God who reigns over all
The Universe! His words are life eternal; they don't fall
On deaf space without bringing results. He speaks with a force,
And life bubbles with vigor. He is existence's origin and source.
What an honor and luck it is to serve such a God!
Life thrives or ceases to exist with His word or nod.

After the angels finish singing, Phanuel poses a question to Christ.

PHANUEL
Lord, why did you place animals on Earth first, if I may ask?
Why not man first? Do animals perform any particular task?

CHRIST
Yes indeed. We want them to make Earth habitable
By balancing nature for man, making it very stable.
We've created Behemoth that'll be called later dinosaur.
Giants will eat up some of them when things get sore.
We'll kill the rest when they become pernicious,
And begin to devour other animals, turning vicious.

We'll put man on Earth when the conditions are in his favor,
To live in her securely, enjoying and relishing her flavor.

FADE OUT.

FADE IN:

INT. IN THE FIFTH HEAVEN, CALLED ARYAM.

After a long period of time, Christ appears at the nursery where the human soul models have been kept and commands them to be alive. They become alive, turning into living entities or souls. They wake up as if from a long slumber. When they are fully alert, they get excited. The angels are happy and flabbergasted. The souls bow before God, and kneeling down, they praise and exalt Him instantly:

Praise be to our God who's made us alive,
To enjoy existence fully, forever to thrive!
No one can steal from us this soul
He has generously granted us all.
O, how wonderful it is indeed to come into existence,
To be aware of being alive, to know of one's essence!
How's it that we are surely able to think and speak,
Endowed with consciousness, be it strong or weak?
How's it that we can look around and become aware
That we, our God and His angels, exist here and there?
Oh, awareness is God's awesome miracle!
Who can explain it save Himself or His oracle?
O, what does life mean, but awareness of one's essence!
O, what truly is reality, but knowledge of one's existence!
We praise you, our Holy God, again and again,
For creating us pure as light, without any stain!

CHRIST
(smiles, pleased with their praise)
Your life will be fabulous filled with incredible adventure.
It'll be exciting, challenging, and involving much venture.
Live with us and be merry, till we give you an intermission
To send you to a nice place called Earth for a noble mission.
(turning to Raguel)
Raguel, take them to the mansions that we've built for each.
Let them eat fruits like papaya, orange, mango, and peach.
Also feed them with milk, honey, and hot cake,
Which, for them, with my mind I just did bake.
Later, show them around heaven. Yes, give them a tour.

RAGUEL
I will do so, my Lord; that's for sure!

Raguel bows and leaves to lead the souls to their respective mansions.

FADE OUT.

FADE IN:

EXT. ARYAM, THE FIFTH HEAVEN.

It is still in Aryam, the Fifth Heaven. After the souls stay in their mansions briefly, Raguel takes them on a tour of the Fifth Heaven. Everything that exists on Earth, and many more things that are not on Earth, are present in the Fifth Heaven. In reality, Earth is a bad replica or distortion of the Fifth Heaven, regardless of the fact that it is patterned after it. If real means indestructible, durable, and eternal, heaven is such, and as such, it is real, though it will be accessed only with a glorified body and not with human body, which was designed to maneuver only three-dimensional earthly reality. Heaven is not a dream. If artificial or fake means destructible or perishable, time-bound and temporal, then Earth is all these things in comparison with heaven, and as such, it is relatively unreal. Earth is the one which is a dream, unless we say that it is real only during our duration on it. It is not the other way around. A good illustration of this are two rings, one of pure gold and the other artificial. The artificial ring pretends to be gold. It is a copy of gold. The gold ring, compared with the artificial, is real, because it is original, indestructible, enduring heat and fire, and lasting infinitely. On the other hand, the artificial ring, which is an imitation of the gold ring, is destructible, burns in fire, and melts away. So, it is not real gold, even though it gives the impression that it is real gold. Therefore, compared with Earth, heaven is more real since it lasts forever.

Everything in Aryam, the Fifth Heaven, which will be the future Kingdom of all those who believe in Jesus Christ, is alive, perfect, conscious, and full of vitality. Animals, and even inanimate objects such as rocks, flowers and rivers have their own awareness and the ability to speak. Furthermore, they are luminous, reflecting colorful lights. Everything in heaven is dazzling with light and colors. There is no waste matter in heaven. Nothing dries up, withers away, or goes out of existence. Most of all, all things are timeless and harmonious with each other. No conflict and strife whatsoever. Only love, peace, patience, wisdom, and tranquility reign here. In fact, the air is pure love. Here, souls breathe love instead of air. Every object releases love as plants release oxygen on Earth. There is no any space for hate. Even the animals, such as the lions and cows, the tigers and goats, and the different birds love one another dearly. They would never think of hurting each other. At this point in time when this story takes place, there are unpopulated towns in heaven, which God had modeled and built with his Word in anticipation of future souls that would fill them in. Later, when the Word becomes Jesus Christ and descends to Earth, He would promise mansions in heaven to those who would believe in Him. It seems that these mansions were or were going to be placed in these towns. The towns are full of rainbow colored flowers that never fade away. Streets bearing the names of God and His holy angels that are paved with gold and precious stones non-existent on Earth, are running throughout heaven. The River of Life and the River of Love flow through them, winding and circling around the towns that are showered by thousands of fountains and waterfalls with hundreds of colors.
Indeed everything in Aryam, the Fifth Heaven, is neat and clean. There is no trash, garbage, or any waste matters whatsoever. The reason for this is simple—everything has been created to last forever without decomposing, decaying, or being wasted, unlike things that are on Earth.
In the beginning, the heavens didn't have any gates. After the rebellion of Lucifer and his followers, however, to keep away the evil angels, God had to order Archangel Gabriel to make a thick wall around Aryam with twelve gates carved out of masses of multicolored pearls, as we saw earlier. Each gate became guarded by twelve warrior angels holding rotating swords of flames.

It is at this point in time that Archangel Raguel takes the fourteen souls on a brief tour of Aryam, the Fifth Heaven. Raguel explains to the souls that God talks to the heavenly natural beings and communicates with them on a regular basis making them aware of the existence of the physical Universe and life in it. Since He has created them with some level of consciousness, they listen to Him and obey Him. That is why when he says, "Wind, blow!" the wind blows. And when He says, "Wind, be still!" the wind becomes still. According to Raguel, Christ has told the rocks, rivers, trees, and animals in heaven about the fate of their counterparts on Earth in the future when it is populated by humans. Therefore, they are aware of the fact that, their counterparts on Earth would suffer from natural catastrophe and man's abuse of planet Earth in the distant future.

MOVING SHOT:

RAGUEL
(pointing at a colorful rock which glitters)
Look at this colorful rock.
It's conscious and can talk.

FIRST SOUL
Really? . . . Can you talk, rock?

ROCK
I'm not mute; of course, I can talk!

SECOND SOUL
Say something.

THE SONG OF THE ROCK
In praise of God I sing and sing,.
What else can I say but exalt and exalt
My God? Once I start, I don't want to halt.
Thank you, Lord, for creating me
Here in heaven, where I've no enemy,
Where the axe won't chisel and sandpapers brush
Me, and the cruel hammer won't pound and crush
Me, where I won't be consumed by a raging and merciless volcano
And be destroyed by earthquake. Nothing ever threatens me. Oh, no!
I am secure here where, without worrying anything will sever
Me, I can live solidly by the grace of my God forever and ever!
And so, in praise of my God I sing and sing,
My whole being adores Him, yes my whole being!

ALL SOULS
Amen! You've a great voice, rock,
Certainly, you can sing and talk!

As soon as they move away from the rock, Raguel leads them to the HALL OF WORSHIP, a colossal edifice, the largest building in the Universe. Externally, it is glittering and quivering as if it was a million stars studded and glued together suspended in the air as geometric shapes and patterns. As soon as they enter it, the fourteen souls feel the presence of God, holiness, love, and peace. The odor of God, which He had left behind, smells like the aroma of a thousand incenses, and wafts in the air. A soft, calming, yet soul-soothing song emanates from all directions created by the nucleus, indeed by the minutest atoms of the walls, the floor, and the ceiling of the edifice. The atoms of the building are actually dancing and praising God for honoring them by allowing them to be His holy temple. It is reminiscent of what Jesus said as He entered Jerusalem sitting on a colt, "If humans don't praise God, surely these stones would." It is designed to hold countless number of angels and souls during holy mass services, which would come into existence over the next millions of years.

On the stage that blazes like yellow, crimson, red, green, violet, and blue flames at the same time, are three thrones made of colorful precious stones surrounded by three perfect circles of rainbows. The center throne belongs to Father God. To its right and left are the thrones of Christ and the Holy Spirit. Lower than that stage is an altar with captivating hues. On the ground floor facing the Holy Stage is a vast and extremely beautiful platform. It is the spot in which the angels praise God.

Archangel Raguel comments on the Hall:

This fabulous hall is the most holy and sacred hall
In the Universe, since in it, God is worshiped by all
Angels and souls in the present and future.
God erected it thus, seeing the big picture.

The souls listen in amazement to the song of the Hall of Worship:

THE SONG OF THE HALL OF WORSHIP
In praise of my God I sing everlastingly! I adore His lordship
For honoring me above other halls of the Universe. I worship
Him in my own way—my atoms leap up with joy to dance
And sing each time they see their God, even if it's a glance.
I was only rock and wood in God's mind in the days of yore.
I'm now a precious work of art, and I'll remain so forevermore.

They step away from the Hall of Worship and stop at a bunch of rainbow colored flowers, which reflect their own luminous lights. They sing in groups sounding like the greatest orchestra in the world. These flowers, like everything else, praise God daily out of their love for Him.

THE SONG OF THE FLOWERS
Hallelujah to our God Almighty!
Who adorned us with such beauty!
Whom has He adorned like us in the whole Universe?
He has made us more beautiful than seas and rivers,

Grasses and leaves, even birds and butterflies.
Let our songs rise high up and echo in the skies.
We shall never fade away, let alone wither away.
Our scent is eternal. It won't vanish even for a day.
Our permanent existence is wholesome and total.
We're immortal, because our Creator is immortal!

ALL SOULS
(to the flowers)
You sing fantastic! You were able our souls to uplift!

THE FLOWERS
We're glad you're uplifted. This is God's gift.

Archangel Raguel then leads the souls to the FOUNTAIN OF HEALING, RIVER OF LIFE, RIVER OF LOVE, and a SINGING BIRD so that the souls can hear their songs.

THE SONG OF FOUNTAIN OF HEALING
In praise of my God I sing,
I'm the fountain of healing.
I flow eternally, gently, yes, gently, without rushing,
I won't vanish like a vapor. I'll be forever gushing
To heal future humans on Earth where I'd be duplicated.
I will heal illnesses, be they simple ones or complicated.
Yeah! I'm clearer than rivers and purer than all springs,
I thank God for all this. In praise of Him, my voice rings.

FIFTH SOUL
O! fountain of healing, indeed you're clear and pure. You're lucky!
You will remain so forevermore. You will never, never be murky!

THE SONG OF THE RIVER OF LIFE
I'm most ancient of rivers, oh, yeah, I'm the first!
I'm the River of Life that can quench all thirst.
I sing unto my God who's the greatest of the great.
I'll never ever dry up, nor do I forever evaporate.

I'll flow and flow, and flow forevermore.
He who drinks from me shall thirst no more.
I'm the most beautiful of rivers with shining and bright
Colors. I'm golden, crimson, green, blue, and honey-light.
I'm most ancient of rivers, oh, yeah, I'm the first!
I'm the River of Life that can quench all thirst.

O! I'll sing and sing eternally, praising my God and Lord.
And when I sing and praise Him lovingly, I'm never bored.

SECOND SOUL
Oh, River of Life, if I can express my whim,
I want to drink of you now, and in you swim!

THE SONG OF THE RIVER OF LOVE
I sing unto my God for keeping me alive,
Forever to love, and forevermore to thrive.
When some beings become hateful later, I'll abate
Their hatred by touching them. Yes, I'll stop hate!
I bubble with love and vigor to cure hate's pain.
He who drinks of me will never hate again.
Any feelings of hatred, I can to love turn.
He who bathes in me will by my love burn.
I sing unto my God for keeping me alive,
Forever to love, forevermore to thrive.

THIRD SOUL
You're great! I can't sing like you, however I strive!

THE SONG OF THE BIRD
Praise be to my God, to my Creator and King
Who beautified me so and enabled me to sing
And to speak. God has generously beautified me. All flowers
Of heaven say I'm more charming than them. My God showers
Upon me lots of blessings. He has made me eternal. I won't die
Forevermore. Spreading my wings proudly, I'll forever fly.
My God gives me the songs I sing, for talent emanates and springs
From Him alone. My voice is sweeter than a harp that sweetly rings.
I praise God with my melody. My throat is a flute that forever sings.

FIRST SOUL
Oh, little bird, your voice's indeed a sweet harp that joy brings,
And in our ears it'll forever and ever ring, even as it now rings.

After stopping at the trees, butterflies, lions, elephants, horses of chariots, and many beautiful other animals that sing and praise God, the souls visit different buildings and mansions serving different purposes. They look from far at God's palace called Palace of Love, a most fantastic building that is as alive as any living being, made of colorful minerals and precious stones beyond human comprehension. They proceed to The Hall of Records where the files of those souls that will be humans in the future are kept alphabetically. Archangel Raguel introduces them to the file system.

RAGUEL

As God is eternal, for Him, everything is in the present,
Existing now and here. For Him, nothing at all is absent.
With this in mind, He has recorded the most exciting history
Of the future now and here. For humans, it will be a mystery.
So, your future on Earth, and your descendants' future
Have been documented and filed by God in a scripture.
This is the House of Records where our God keeps a file
For each of you, which grows as your needs and deeds pile
Up. The records indicate probabilities and possibilities
As well as actual occurrences, events, and solid realities.
God has recorded them ahead of time to handle each
Of your cases in the future, to guide you and also teach
You in visions and dreams, to inspire your achievements,
To meet your needs and contribute to your improvements.
Your life on Earth someday when our God sanctions
Your stay there, are herein recorded: all your actions
Or inactions, which make you accountable
For your deeds, reflecting why you were able
Or unable to achieve your goals in different instances,
In a given period of time and particular circumstances.
You can look at them, but I'm not authorized to open
Them. Presently, only our God knows what'll happen.

After this, Archangel Raguel opens a chamber within the innermost part of the Hall of Records and points to two gigantic GOLDEN BOOKS that are sealed completely and shelved in a transparent closet.

RAGUEL
(pointing at the two books from a distance)
As you see, there are two untouchable books in here—
The Book of Life and Book of Death, inspiring fear.
Names of all humans who'll walk on Earth's surface
Are written in these books. They'll come face to face
With God at the world's end
To receive a reward to spend
Eternity in heaven with God or be destroyed in the Lake of Fire
With Lucifer the vicious, who did fall because of his vain desire.
Those written in the Book of Life will receive life eternal.
Those written in the Book of Death receive death infernal.

After the souls have an exterior glimpse of their files, Raguel shows them HEAVEN'S LIBRARY.

RAGUEL

Look, this is the main library of heaven. All these wonderful books
Detail the future history of Earth and the Universe. When one looks
At them intently in order to understand a subject,
The subject runs through the mind as an object,
And you can comprehend it fully in its totality,
Without even opening it for a second in reality.
Whatever history humans will make, that history
Is already recorded truthfully, clearing the mystery.
Just by being present in here, you'll know the future
And the past of the Universe and of every creature.

As they walk on the streets of heaven bearing the names of God and the angels, stepping on the golden and precious stones, they come across a street which once used to be called "Lucifer Boulevard." The street is faded and deserted now. Raguel makes a remark.

RAGUEL

This street used to be called "Lucifer Boulevard."
It was beautiful and magnanimous by any standard.
Lucifer's name, as you see right here, is sadly faded.
The street is deserted, though with gold embedded.
That's exactly what will happen to your memorial
When you disobey God and become conspiratorial.

From there, Raguel takes them to the HOUSE OF HUMAN SPARE PARTS and enlightens them.

RAGUEL

God's highly organized. He plans everything in advance,
Though He could also be spontaneous doing things at once.
Since He knows humans will someday need body parts,
He has stored them here in abundance. The storage starts
(pointing with his sword)
Right here and goes all the way up to the end of the wall.
They're like sunlight here but tangible on Earth for all.
Whenever people will pray for miraculous healings,
God will use these for the missing parts, as fillings.

When they come out of the House of Human Parts, Raguel reveals to them the hall in which the fruits of the Spirit are kept in colorful bottles.

RAGUEL
(pointing at different bottles)
These colorful bottles that you see consist of different dosages
Of the fruits of the Spirit humans will need in different ages,

Such as love, joy, patience, longsuffering, wisdom, perseverance,
Faith, kindness, trust, loyalty, meekness, spirituality, and tolerance.
When men will pray to receive these gifts honestly,
God will open the bottles and give them earnestly.

ONE OF THE SOULS
(looking around)
Raguel, once you said the sun lightens Earth's ground.
How come heaven is so lighted? There's no sun around.

RAGUEL
Here light emanates from our Good Lord.
His floodlight is all over heaven poured.
Besides, everything in heaven including myself and you
Glows amazingly and colorfully reflecting light in lieu
Of the sun. But when the Lord God and all of us rest,
The light becomes soothing and mellower, which's best
For relaxation, meditation, and retreat,
As it's without much brightness and heat.

After a while, you'll learn how to do things at will.
Your own thoughts have power in heaven to fulfill
Your wishes and desires. When you're in a great mood
To have a tasty food, just by wishing, you can have food.
By desiring to be in a wood, you will find yourself in a wood.
Just by reflecting a bit, you can certainly have anything good.
If you don't want to, you don't have to eat or drink.
You get hungry or thirsty if you decide so to think.
Some of us eat and drink just for the taste of the treat.
Otherwise, it's not really necessary to drink or eat.

FADE OUT.

FADE IN:

EXT. EL-SHADAI OR SHADAYA, THE SEVENTH HEAVEN THAT BEARS GOD'S NAME.

Millions of years pass by and God decides to eliminate some of the perverted Behemoth (dinosaurs) and other ferocious animals to place man on Earth.

CHRIST
It's about time a few of the ferocious Behemoths to obliterate.
They're eating up plants and even animals, at an alarming rate.
The vicious Behemoths and humans can't live in harmony together.
I'll leave the harmless ones that wear scary feathers for the weather.
A little while after the horrible Behemoths are dead and gone,
My beloved man will rule the world sitting in a majestic throne.
I'm now going to strike the Earth with a very light asteroid,
To remove some of the Behemoths and make their threat void.
Sadly, someday, when those evil beings from out of space who're distinct,
abduct women, they father giants who'd kill the rest, making them extinct.

Christ strikes the perverted and dangerous Behemoths with an asteroid, and obliterates them, sparing the harmless ones to live with humans. Unfortunately, according to the Ethiopian book of creation known as Djan Shoa, the so-called sons of God who were actually malicious, extraterrestrial beings from the world known as Memros, came to Earth by spacecraft and took the daughters of men as wives by force. They were ugly and unlike humans. Giants who were extremely hungry all the time were born as a result of this illegal genetic mixing. These hungry giants ate everything up including humans and animals. Being inhumanly strong and ferocious hunters, they killed in groups and ate up the remaining behemoths, which we identify today as Dinosaurs. God had to destroy with the "Flood of Noah" these giants and humans that had caused much havoc and bloodshed on Earth.

After the harmful behemoths (Dinosaurs) are eliminated, Earth rests briefly and God becomes ready to create humans, the apex of His creation, in the first Earth Age. Before Christ sends human souls to earth, The Holy Trinity talk to them about it. They are the fourteen souls with no gender.

CHRIST
My beloved children, I need your full attention and focus.
We're holding with you right now a conference to discuss
Your future. It's about time that you go down to Earth.
As I told you all in the past, it will be like another birth.

The souls cry fearing the uncertain future on Earth. Their tears run down their cheeks.

FIRST SOUL
Lord, we're very happy here. We don't want to go to Earth!
We were born in heaven. We really don't want another birth!

FATHER GOD
(moved by their reaction)
Beloved, you've to be brave hence;
And your future joy will be immense.

HOLY SPIRIT
Believe us dear, we won't do to you anything unfair,
Whatever we want you to do is for your own welfare.

SECOND SOUL
Lord God, here in heaven, we're content and feel great.
Earthly life seems uncertain filled with unknown threat.

CHRIST
The result will be good though in the beginning it may be hard.
We won't forsake you. And our dear angels will be your guard.
Earthly life is necessary for your growth though it lacks much leisure.
You may be sad there, but it's with sorrow only that you do measure
Joy. You'll appreciate more the happiness in heaven, after you roam
On Earth, go through thick and thin down there and come back home.
There are lots of things to learn on Earth, which can't be learned
In heaven. If you endure, great is the final reward to be earned.
Children, we've to test your free will, faith, loyalty, and obedience.
We'll guide you. If you pray fervently, we'll grant you audience.
We've to erase your memory of heaven at birth,
So that it doesn't interfere with your task on Earth.
We'll endow you with different talents: some with dance, poetry,
And music, others with science, math, engineering, and pottery.
Trust us our children, the end result will be wonderful. Be cheerful!
It'll be great, though it may now seem very hard, gloomy, and fearful.

THIRD SOUL
Are you sure you will return us home at last
From Earth where we'll be like an outcast?

HOLY SPIRIT
It depends on yourselves. If you walk with us, we'll listen to your plea,
And pave your way. You'll return straight to us like the river to the sea.
Looking into your future, we see all of you won't stray in any way.
But sadly, some of your seeds will consciously choose to stay away.
You will come back triumphantly, eligible for heavenly admission.
We'll be proud of you for successfully accomplishing your mission.

CHRIST
To save your seeds, we will form a man called Adam later. Abraham
Will be his son. I'll be born from him and save the children of Adam,
And your children as well, many, many years
Hence, when Earth is flooded by blood and tears.

FOURTH SOUL
I hope we'll come back home very soon
To receive from you our heavenly boon.

FATHER GOD
Yes, since what on Earth is a thousand years even
Is like one day, right here in our timeless heaven.

ALL SOULS
We trust our God! He'll neither forsake nor abandon
Us! Our God is good and just! May His will be done!

The Holy Trinity kiss sadly all the fourteen souls one by one.

CHRIST
(to the souls)
One half of you will be female, the other half male, when you dwell
On Earth. Whether you be male or female, you'll all perform well.
Thus, by being male and female, you can give birth
To children whose seeds will forever fill the Earth.

FATHER GOD
Fear not, my children. You'll all do well.

ALL SOULS
Farewell to our God, farewell!

CHRIST
(with a loud and reverberating voice)
Oh, ye souls, wear flesh, and be human,
So that you can accomplish our plan.
Wear bodies made of earth, wind, water, and fire!
May Earth obey you to fulfill your hearts' desire!

*The fourteen souls are created as seven male and female human beings in Ethiopia, which
was then like paradise, harmonious and suitable, indeed ideal, for human existence and
development. The Holy Trinity and the angels see this from heaven and are very delighted.
The newly created humans too are very happy to be on Earth as they look around and see the
superb beauty which encompasses them. Shortly after, Christ and His angels follow them to*

Earth. Surprisingly enough, invisible to the newly created men and women but visible to the host of heaven, Lucifer and his fallen angels are watching them with great wonder and curiosity. The men and women sing and praise God immediately:

ALL MEN AND WOMEN
Glory be unto our God; for Him nothing is impossible.
We were invisible beings, but He has made us visible.
He created and adorned Earth meticulously for our sake.
He loves us much. Yes, no force would His love shake.
The earth and sea and the sky with its glory,
He made for our joy. They're His love story.
Let us rejoice and worship forever our God.
For uniting each soul with each fabulous bod.

CHRIST
Multiply in number and rule this planet.
If you love and adore me, like a magnet
Your love, loyalty, and obedience will draw me towards
You. If you observe my commandments, your rewards
Will be great. You shall worship no other gods but me.
To worship anyone besides me is to worship my enemy.
(gazing at Lucifer who is standing nearby)
And Lucifer is my enemy. He's a fallen and disgraced
Angel who hates us all, whose evil deeds could be traced
To heaven when he did attempt vainly to usurp my place,
Misleading many angels that I had to cast out of my face.
He and his angles will try vainly to seduce and entice
You to practice witchcraft, pretending to be very nice,
Appearing like angels of light and promising what they can't deliver
To get you into the Lake of Fire, which can melt instantly solid silver
And gold. Be watchful incessantly lest they craftily ensnare
You, O! my beloved, catching you off guard and unaware.
If you indeed walk with me steadily in life every inch,
If you observe my commandments and don't flinch,
You'll inherit eternal life and come back home
Alive to join me in heaven when you stop to roam
About earth, having lived a long life of leisure,
Enjoying everything I created for your pleasure.
Make sure that they don't divide and push you to abandon
Each other. Should that happen, it's your end. You're done!
Eventually, as you grow in useful experience and number,
You'll achieve mighty civilizations which would encumber
You very heavily if you stray away from me,
If you abuse your power and serve my enemy.

Should that happen, sadly, I've to obliterate without trace
You and your civilizations, to replace you with another race.

As Ethiopia the birth place of man becomes too crowded,
Even as the heavens are with uncountable stars studded,
Some will move away to be other races over millions of years
Due to climatic conditions, after so much bloodletting and tears.

ALL THE PEOPLE
We'll be watchful, and we'll never associate
With the fallen angels, even if they initiate
Contact with us. We'll keep your commandment.
We will stick together lest we face disbandment.

CHRIST
Initially, our angels will teach you to till these lands,
to build houses as well us roads, with tools and hands.

A bunch of working angels start teaching the people how to till land, build houses and roads.
Lucifer, who is now Satan, runs after Christ and prostrates before Him shaking in fear. He
speaks after he overcomes his fear.

LUCIFER
Lord God, can I have your permission
To launch now my vicious mission?

CHRIST
(stunned and angry)
How quick you are, eh! Satan, to destroy
My wonderful creation and steal my joy!
I've built a thick wall around my newly born babies.
Wait a while before trying to drag them into an abyss.

(pause)

LUCIFER
Azazel, Ananya, Semazya and even I beg your pardon
For every wrong deed, which we've previously done.

CHRIST
This is astonishing…What does it mean in reality?

LUCIFER
We miss heaven. We want to return to heaven in actuality.

89

CHRIST
(knowing full well they won't repent)
Repent before we discuss the possibility.

LUCIFER
After all those years of loitering we've spent
Outside heaven, it's extremely hard to repent.

CHRIST
If you don't want to repent, you won't be forgiven,
Nor will you be allowed to come back to heaven.

LUCIFER
If we've no any hope of ever returning
To heaven, our only alternative is to turn
Away from you more and more and commit
Horrendous wickedness without any limit.

CHRIST
I presume that's how
It will be as of now.

(pause)

Christ prophecies the fate of the fallen angels and the future of the world. As indicated earlier, since God is in eternal presence, He sees things that have not yet occurred as if they are happening now or have already taken place. Therefore, His speech is at times in the present tense. The fallen angels don't understand everything God says, but they listen any way, in amazement. When He speaks of the 20th or the 21st Centuries, for instance, he may employ vocabularies, terms, jargons and idiomatic expressions that are typical of the times, such as computer, technology, Television, etc.. He repeats himself at times to impress his sayings on the mind of the fallen angels who don't yet comprehend some of them despite their incredible mental power to understand things in the abstract. Christ addresses Lucifer most of the time, even though what He prophecies applies to all of them.

CHRIST
You won't understand everything I'll say now about your evil venture;
However, when you get involved in it, you'll understand it in the future.
I'll just tell you a few of the main events that will involve
You in the future, when I allow them to unfold and evolve.
Your life history will be complex, long and problematic
I'll focus only on your last days as they will be dramatic.
There maybe words and terms that I'll use that represent
The times under discussion, that you won't grasp at present.
Don't worry about that. Just
Listen, meditate and digest. .

There'll be different civilizations on Earth that'd be flawless
Until you corrupt their founders, thus making them lawless,
Godless, oppressive, tyrannical, and inventors of explosives,
That'll will annihilate them, making them numb and passives
To my pleas and warnings. Consequently, I shall wipe them all out
From the surface of the Earth when they traverse on the wrong rout.

After I destroy Earth with a torrential rain that'll be called the Flood
Of Noah, one of Noah's descendants will follow you to shed blood,
Create a "mystery religion" in Babylon, and defiantly build a tower
To reach my heights inspired by you. Like you, at the peak of power,
He'll demand worship, and he, his wife and son will be worshipped
By his subjects. His name is Nimrod. Later, he will be whipped
And beaten by me. I'll demolish his tower of contempt,
Confusing his masons, and frustrating his vicious attempt.

(looking in Lucifer's eyes)
Unfortunately, the religion you'll establish through him will last
Secretly, till my return to Earth to devastate it forever like a blast.
Many will worship you through this religion indeed till my return
To destroy you and your worshippers, when I, with rage burn.
Misleading uncountable humans, you'll pervert multitude,
That, though I created them, towards me harbor ill-attitude.
You'll, regrettably, possess and pervert them so much by being my usurper,
That when you say I, the Christ, am Satan, and you're God Adonai, a Super
And sovereign God, they will believe you. And when you deceive
Them vowing you'll make them gods and goddesses, they'll receive
You in stupor with open arms, and worship you. Since you revolted
Against us seeking adulation and worship, you'll have them unbolted
And unabated. Nevertheless, you and your worshipers shall pay
A huge price for all this during my inevitable Judgment Day.

At the end of the world, as my Day of Judgment approaches,
You'll raise a nefarious person you'll use. One that encroaches
The freedom of all, demanding worship; a maniac whose thirst
For power and blood is boundless. He'll be called the Anti Christ.
He'll conquer, seize craftily, and subdue more than half
Of the world with his charm and army, on your behalf.
He does so with the help of one of your false prophets that generates
For him recognition. He'll destroy many nations as he concentrates
Power in his hand. He will forcefully put the mark of his name
On your followers' hands and foreheads at the apex of his fame.
You'll give a deadline for all human beings to take

The Mark of the Beast, putting their lives at stake.
You'll use hunger as a weapon to brutally subdue
Those that refuse to take your mark after the due
Date. They won't be able to buy food from the store.
You'll starve them to death mercilessly, therefore.

Those who want to stay alive will surely take your mark,
Confirming that they are yours. There souls will be dark
For trading their precious souls for bread.
You'll possess them, and they'll all head
To hell. However, the wise and the brave will jealously cherish
Their souls, knowing that, sooner or later, their bodies will perish.
The souls of those braves you kill for not taking your Satanic mark
Will live with me forever in heaven, singing in glee like the skylark.

Possessing him totally and dwelling in him for seven human years,
You'll turn the world upside down, shedding much blood and tears,
Until I interfere and stop you saying "enough is enough! Halt!"
Then the world shall know I'm Almighty God, and only me exalt!
I'll cast the false Christ and prophet into the horrible Lake of fire,
Where they'll burn. You'll join them later after serving what I desire. .

There will be numerous human beings who'll hate
Me like you have hated me, at the appointed date
And time, in the distant, distant future.
You and they'll have the same nature.
You'll use these earthlings to hurt me and to do evil,
Someday when you begin to be called Satan, the Devil.
Among them are insane individuals that think they're wittler,
Called Adam Weishaupt, Karl Marx, Lenin, Stalin and Hitler.

To start from the last, this vicious man, Hitler, who's mentally cripple,
Will be maneuvered by you to eliminate millions of my chosen people,
Who, unfortunately, will stray away from me...(*pause*) yeah...
Because you'll mislead them to think I'm the false messiah.
Your children, who're merchants of war will wickedly finance
Him so that they can loan money to all the fighters, and advance
And maximize their profit also by constructing the ruins of war.
They gain tons of money from selling weapons. All this, I abhor.

Adam Weishaupt will try to serve me in the beginning
As a priest. Then he'll turn against me evilly meaning
To willfully lure away my priests and children I adore.
He does so influenced by you when he opens the door

Of his heart to you. You'll enter it to beat with his heartbeat,
Which he, maliciously enjoys, considering this to be neat.
You'll make him and his followers to vainly take over
The world for you through deception and some endeavor.
You'll inspire him to write books to discredit me, and in order
To marginalize me and my followers, to destroy the order
Of society, cause much bloodshed, lawlessness, grief, and turmoil,
Exploiting the goodwill and emotion of angry youngsters that toil
To bring about change, which sadly, would make things
Worst when they topple over their queens and kings.

Disguised as my priest in a country called Germany,
He'll unleash havoc in France, that'd annihilate many.
You shall deceive him a great deal. You'll instill
In his mind and heart those very words that still
Reverberate here in heaven, such as "liberty, equality
And fraternity", which are impossible to attain, in reality,
As long as you are their champion, and you are around.
It's only I who can bring about these after you're bound.

These words will inspire the emotional youth, and for sure,
The oppressed and wretched of the earth that sadly endure.
A lot of suffering, to revolt, thinking they'll serve justice.
Tragically, the result of such revolts will be evil practice.
Truly, these are the same words with which you were able
To entice against us our angels that were naive and gullible.

Weishaupt, the evil-genius, will instruct your men to syndicate
The media so as to control the mind of the populace and dictate
What they should subliminally digest and consume.
Many will be enslaved mentally, though they assume
They're free. The masses will never find out through the net-works
Of the media your quiet plots to take over the planet. All this irks
Me...Even children will be brainwashed being taught falsehood
To make them atheists and evolutionists, and refute my Godhood.

Karl Marx, Lenin, and Stalin will follow
Him because you'll influence their hollow
Hearts to launch against me and their rulers violent revolutions
That would shed an ocean of blood without bringing solutions
To the problems of the people that suffer under tyranny's yoke
Only I, am able to deliver them if they ask me. Yours is a joke.

Even though they lie to the masses denying God and the existence
Of Satan, they'll consult and worship you secretly with persistence.
They'll be members of an underground group called secret society,
In which you and your children conspire against God Almighty.
You'll initiate them in here, give them instructions to renounce
God, sacrifice for you, worship you, and plan and announce
The atrocities they'll commit in cold blood against their fellow
Men, including revolutions, wars, and the aftermaths that follow.
All the major leaders of world revolutions and wars will surely be regular
Members of your secret societies plotting against their citizens in particular.
They'll stir up the oppressed and use them as cannon fodders to seize power
In their name, oppress them more, erase their faith in me, and make life sour.

When Karl Marx is a boy, he'll adore me much and compose
Poems that praise me. After you meet him, he'll start to oppose
Me. You'll meet him in college where your group, a Satanic
Group, will recruit him. He'll be the rest of his life a titanic,
Devout Satanist that worships you in secret willing to be used
By you. In the name of liberty, equality and justice for the abused
And the downtrodden, he'll promote communism,
Championing class struggle with a big enthusiasm.
To bring about bloody revolutions, and vowing to dethrone
Me from heaven, shaking his fist and body with angry tone.
Later, he will dare say, "religion is the opiate of the poor."
But it's rather Marxism that becomes their opiate, for sure.
Yet, being two-faced, he'll serve as a high priest of your
Religion and worship you with devotion until he dies,
Making the unsuspecting world to believe in his lies.

(pause)

What's ironic is that, you're the one that'll harden rulers, for sure,
And make them insensitive to the plight of the poor that endure.
Then you'll turn around and entice the poor and young
To rebel against their tyrannical rulers, to hack or hang
Them, or to kill them in any fashion or inhuman manner.
Anything you lead is evil, though you carry a good banner.
You know deep down inside that you don't care
A bit for the poor or for any human welfare.
All you'll do is exploit human resentment to cause blood spilling,
Lawlessness, godlessness, perversion, and indiscriminate killing.
Your desire is to continuously create havoc and anarchy,
So that you can place your throne on top of the hierarchy.

AZAZEL
It is true, Lord God, he wanted to destroy your hierarchy
To replace it with strife, disorderliness and total anarchy,
So that he could sit on top of us all in a new hierarchy.

CHRIST
We knew before we formed him long, long time ago,
That he'd wish to do so because of his insatiable ego.

(to Lucifer)

You know hierarchy is vertical, going from top to bottom. Anarchy
Is horizontal, lawless, chaotic, uncontrollable, and anti monarchy.
It serves you well. That's why you rebelled against our hierarchy.
No doubt you'll do the same on Earth someday in alliance
With your evil men who will obey you in compliance.

(pause)

You create problems yourself, and bring forth their solutions,
Which are worst than the problems. Thus, waves of revolutions
And wars break one after another, unleashing malady after malady,
And making the good Earth a stage of tragedy after tragedy,
Which, when repeated endlessly, feels like comedy after comedy.

Joseph Stalin will start attending a Jesuit seminary
Pretending to serve me as a priest and missionary
Until the time when he joins a Satanic communist, underground
Group where he meets Lenin and they deny my existence around
Earth and the universe, and the fact that I created everything.
This evil, merciless man, will suspect and fear even his own shadow
And purge millions of men, making every Russian woman a widow.

Vladimir Lenin curses me and tramples upon my cross in disdain.
A Satanic group of bankers will smuggle him to Russia in a train
From Switzerland to implement Weishaupt's evil mission, and to launch
An experimental revolution in Russia, and not in Switzerland. A staunch
Atheist just like his idol Karl Marx, Vladimir Lenin would infect
The world with atheism negating our existence with his intellect,
And launch a brutal carnage on poor Russia called the "Red Terror",
In which he and his associates shall murder millions in untold horror. .
Towards the end of his life, you'll paralyze him, and he will howl
And bay at the moon like an agonized wolf because of your fowl
Play on him after you make him suffer from syphilis and madness,
Torturing him with guilt and remorse, and striking him with sadness.

95

Though all these men descend from Abraham biologically, actually
They share some of your characters, and are your children spiritually.
The revolutions you and they wage will be called "Jewish revolution"
All Jews shouldn't be blamed because a few make a wicked resolution
And create more discord and calamity claiming to provide a solution.

To the genuine children of Abraham, these men's deed is a big damage,
For it'll make them seem to be evil, and will tarnish their good image.
I love righteous Abraham, because, unlike his relatives, he'll refuse
To worship you. He'll be obedient to me. You cannot easily confuse
Him like you do others. His faith in me is immeasurable. He is kind.
I've decided to be born from his loins someday to save humankind.
I've promised him that, though his remnants offend me, I won't forsake
Them completely; not that they deserve my mercy, but only for his sake.

In order to profit from the proceeds of wars,
And to eliminate populations in the course
Of the wars, most of all, to steal the world by sword and spear
When men suffer from the result of war, and are stricken by fear,
Your children will wage three world wars unleashing carnage,
In a futile attempt to form a world government in the last age.
The Third World War will shatter Earth to pieces with modern
Weapons. I've to intrude to punish you and yours. I'm very stern.

Sadly, these individuals and you, will mislead millions promising
Paradise, and inflicting untold death all over the world, dismissing
My teachings of non-violence, peace and love, and my commandment
Not to kill. Moreover, jealous of my future kingdom and government,
As I said, you'll vainly attempt to establish a Satanic, world government,
To unleash unthinkable havoc and pain in a grimy, demonic environment.

LUCIFER
I can't imagine myself being my God's rival!

CHRIST
You are my rival already; and you'll be even more at my earthly arrival.

You'll follow my trail everywhere to ruin my work, and to steal
The souls of the people I love most and treasure a great deal.
You'll lure my chosen ones to worship you on the hills
Of Israel. Sadly, they'll sacrifice for you and practice ills.
They'll spark my wrath and I'll raise against them from Babylon
King Nebuchadnezzar to enslave them seeing their heart's swollen.
He'll drive them in chains and humiliation to the cursed Babylon

Where you'll teach them witchcraft and its ritual
Called Kabala for seventy years. This is the actual
Mystery Religion of the Babylonians Nimrod will establish,
Building the tower of contempt, which we will demolish.

After I've mercy on my people and free them from their captivity,
They'll settle around the world and engage in religious activity.
They'll continue to practice Kabala and worship you behind
My back thinking I won't see them, as if I am deaf and blind.
You'll use some of these Kabalistic men like Adam Weishaupt, Lenin,
Karl Marx, who'll be your high priest, Trotsky, and that Joseph Stalin.
Sadly, your Babylonian Mystery Religion or the Kabala, will
Be rampant among Abraham's children and do appalling ill,
Your devilish desire to fulfill,
Against my divine will...
These Kabalistic, communistic individuals are your fronts men.
The engines behind these will be your invisible Kabalists then.
These hidden Kabalists will be very wealthy and of noble birth,
Who, to please you and serve you obediently, will ruin my Earth.

These same men, who are in truth supposed
To be Abraham's children, will be opposed
To Abraham's God, and support and finance Hitler for profit
So that he'd eradicate their own people considering them unfit
To live in this world. These bestial creatures have thick skin.
They adore you, and love money more than God and their kin.
Sadly, because of their ill deeds, people will blame all
The children of Abraham, who themselves take the toll.
It's like blaming the dead victim instead
Of the culprit that caused him to be dead.
Yes indeed, these are the same group of greedy
Men who'd loan Lenin money to wage a speedy
Revolution in poor Russia, so that he'd pay them back fourfold.
Indeed, he'll pay them back with much interest as he'd been told.
It's the same sort of men that claim descent from Abraham, that'll lay
A trap for me at the prime of my life, to mercilessly and unjustly slay
Me. They aren't any different than assassins that their victims waylay.

(turning to the other angels)

All of you will blend into human societies and ride humans like horse.
You'll live in them like a house to make their lives from worst to worse.
You'll assimilate and acculturate in every culture and civilization;
To launch on your quiet destruction, numbing men's realization.

(facing Lucifer)

Earth's great men—kings and nobles, will prostrate secretly before you,
Though they make their citizens prostrate before them in plain view.
Infiltrating their governments invisibly and speaking their languages,
You'll control their leaders and misguide their affairs in all the ages.
When your last days of power diminish and get numbered,
Humans will be by your bloody activities encumbered.
You'll certainly form organizations
That will unite the world's nations
As a first step to establish
One world government and your religion. This, you'll accomplish
Through deception, until my return your government to demolish,
To herald the advent of my kingdom that will dry blood and tears,
Eradicating injustice, war, wickedness, greed, hate, death and fears.

You'll divert men's attention so that they'll focus only on leisure,
And on the pursuit for worldly knowledge, good only for pleasure
And comfort. This way, they'll forget that I've placed them on Earth,
To seek and worship me, and live with me in heaven, in a new birth.
You and your impious man will demand worship in my Holy City.
When my people refuse, you'll rush to persecute them without pity.
In the end, you'll march to wipe out all of my people with your army.
I'll obliterate your army and save my kin though they'd crucified me.
When they realize it was me their God they'd rejected and killed,
They'll wail and moan greatly for my innocent blood they'd spilled.

Lucifer gets stunned.

LUCIFER
Kill who?...you?....crucify?

CHRIST
Yes, kill me....crucify
Me... justice to satisfy...

(Continuing after a brief moment of silence)

Your evil schemes are not limited to Earth. You'll corrupt those
Intelligent beings that live on a distant world called Memrose.
You'll inspire them to fly their spaceships to Earth to forcefully mate
With women, to ruin my plan, and to see the result after they copulate.
Ugly giants that reach the heavens will be born in violation of my plan;
Since I had never intended aliens to have sex with any woman or man.

These illegitimate giants that'll be born like that become a disaster
That'd destroy Earth. I'll sink them and the whole world under water.

I'll grant you and your children so much power, so that those that hate
Me, hate me more, and those that love me, love me more, until the date,
That appointed date, arrives suddenly as lighting in due time, and I toss
You and your children into a Fiery Lake Then all will know I'm the boss.
But before that time, you and yours shall inflict incalculable carnage
On those who love me and my chosen people, till I destroy you in rage.
Later, you'll use such aliens and their technology to deny and undermine
Me, to make all worship the False Christ, except those that are mine.
Beginning in their mothers' wombs some will be mine and blessed.
Others will be yours, cursed from the start and absolutely messed
Up. Yours are born for hate and strife.
Mine, for pure love and peaceful life.
Yours are written in that scary *Book of Death*. Mine,
In the *Book of Life*, to fulfill my design that's divine.

Christ pauses for a second. Lucifer looks at him in amazement mixed with fear.

It was for the joy of my beloved man that I formed
The Earth. But you'll take it when it's by sin stormed.
Though I love him tenderly, man will sin the day you tempt
Him to sin against me. You'll surely succeed in your attempt.
You'll rule the world until I descend to Earth to lay
Down the foundations of my Kingdom. But I'll delay
This, all this, until the horrific last days of the world when
Yours is no longer necessary to advance my cause then.

I bequeathed man the world for free. When you mess him up without delay,
Man will sell to man everything. For instance, he'll charge a lot every day
For heat and light. If I were to charge for my sun, who can afford to pay?
I provide food and water. Man sells. If I demand payment, who could pay?
Humans won't thank me for any of my free gifts, but grab them everyday.

MICHAEL
(in his heart)
Evil Lucifer will rule beautiful Earth? Wow!
Is he getting appointed for rebelling? How?...

CHRIST
(to Michael)
Dear Michael, this is neither appointment,
Nor promotion. It's a tough assignment,
To pave the way for my earthly government.

LUCIFER
If you want me to accomplish all these, some of which are hard,
O, Lord God, for serving you obediently, what's my final reward?

CHRIST
What more reward is there for you when you retire,
O, Satan, than that long-awaited, red-hot, Lake of Fire?

(pause)

I've assigned you to be king over the kings of the Earth,
And you'll be called the "ruler of the world" until my birth
On Earth to divide your kingdom with my mighty, divine
Power. You won't have dominion over those who'll be mine.
Until then and till the establishment of my Earthly Kingdom,
You'll rule and influence world leaders that reject me. Seldom
Will you be able to control leaders that love me and pray
To me for guidance in worship and adulation every day.

Some of the fallen angels will be princes representing your
Kingdom. They'll influence all the nations invisibly, for sure.
Your scheme of snaring human beings to get them to hell is simple—-
You'll offer fleeting things like money, fame, and power; and people
Of the world will flock behind you in obedience and disgrace.
Though they'll lose their souls eternally for these, they'll race
To gain them. But those few that are mine and wise
Will spit upon all these traps, and above them rise.

LUCIFER
But how can I offer money
To men, when I don't have any?

CHRIST
Your worshipers who'll have tons of money
All over the world, will surely be many.
You'll give others their money.
You'll have prominent men who are like you. Among them are actors.
And singers called stars, bankers, judges, priests, senators, contractors,
Statesmen, brokers, traders, writers, journalists, soldiers of high ranks,
And police chiefs. You'll own world financial institutions and banks.
You'll have illicit drug monies, which your children in higher positions
Will launder to use for wicked undertakings and run your evil institutions.
Your children in higher echelons, besides filling their coffer and vault
With drug funds, they'll use the drugs to numb the youth not to revolt.

They'll be the ones that distribute tons of drugs clandestinely, protected well
By the law. Yet, they'll incarcerate the poor for selling a bit or intending to sell.
Though outwardly these prominent figures of society and governments
Seem to worship me, they serve you secretly breaking my commandments.
You'll also utilize their monies and financial institutes to control at bay
Poor countries. You'll loan their corrupt rulers monies they can't pay
Back, to confiscate their natural resources and dictate and impose
Your policies on them, as long as they submit and don't oppose. .

At one point in time, you'll abolish coin and all paper money
To totally nationalize the financial system and to inflict agony
Upon those who'll resist your devilish one world economic system.
You'll enforce electronic exchange system with a great momentum.
Initially you'll introduce credit cards. Your real, successful spell
And control over men will be when you force them to buy and sell
With computer chips you'll implant under their skin. You will kill
Those who resent it. I'll save their souls to avenge the blood you spill.

*Lucifer raises his eyebrows in bewilderment, unable to comprehend most of the incredible
things his God is saying.*

European nations will surrender their sovereignty to you under the excuse
Of unification. And you'll empower your charismatic, False Christ to use
The European nations as your launch-pad to take
And swallow the rest of the world like a piece of cake.
You'll intoxicate and charm all Europe with your magical powers,
And with the charisma of your False Christ, that among them towers.
In their euphoric stupor, they'll reject me, and flirt with you for hours.

You'll charm men even if you do nothing, but materialize supernaturally
Before them. They'll get stunned, frightened, mesmerized, and rally
Around you, unaware that they are playing with fire,
Bounded and entangled by your invisible lethal wire.
Add to this your angels that set traps to men, preoccupied with them fully,
Unlike my angels who find it hard to approach them when men are unholy.

(pause)

In the latter days, there'll be lots of good and evil scientific inventions
And technological discoveries against which there won't be preventions.
You'll use them recklessly to control over men, to attain
All the whim of your heart, power to gain, and to retain.
You'll fill with cameras the streets and buildings, that in all moments
Trace individuals' private lives, personal activities and movements.

The whole atmosphere will be jammed by electronic devices
That eye on people and help you embark on fully your vices.
You'll inject forcefully each person's forehead or right hand
With a computer-attached chip as small as a grain of sand.
There'll be a central monster computer called "The Beast",
That monitors humans around the world, be they in the East
Or West. The images—the pictures, portraits and busts of your False
Christ will be on televisions, screens, posters, billboards and walls,
And men will be coerced to prostrate before them and worship
Them, be they small, big, common, or in positions of leadership.
At that time, your insatiable fantasy will run amok,
Even though now, to you, it seems to be a mock.

LUCIFER
(in his heart)
Since my life's desire is to be worshiped, I don't care if I burn in the Lake
Of Fire, after I get worshiped by all men through the Christ, which's fake.

CHRIST
(hearing his heart)
You say so now, but you'll prove yourself a liar,
When you're immersed deep in the Lake of Fire.

LUCIFER
O! Almighty God, when my end comes, please do me one favor—
Don't burn me and torture me in that Lake of Fire forever and ever,
I beseech you my Creator, have mercy on me, by doing me this favor—
Dissolve me in the fire so that I won't remember or feel anything ever.

CHRIST
At the right hour and minute, in order fairly justice to serve,
We will give all you rebels, the exact sentence you deserve.

(pause)

Meanwhile I'll need you to test for me each and all,
By being to all a formidable hurdle and a thick wall.
Those that overcome you shall receive the welcome of a hero
In heaven. The success sum of those that'll worship you is zero.
Even though I am the only starter and finisher of salvation,
My angels will give my children who overcome you an ovation .
I will be proud of them before my angels, and they'll be proud
Of their persistent walk with me. My angels will sing this loud.

LUCIFER
Who'll have more children after what's said and done, in a nut
Shell? I mean after your grand plan is carried out in life's gamut?

CHRIST
Of course, you will have more children, without if and but.

LUCIFE
How so, if I may enquire?

CHRIST
Because, narrow is the road to heaven, and broad to the Lake of Fire.
Indeed, narrow and windy, and thorny and cliffy, is the road
To everlasting life; and to that of eternal death—very broad.

LUCIFER
Which of my religions will serve me most?

CHRIST
In those that flatly deny my absolute Godhood, many shall be lost.
Your religions filled with rituals, that preach that there are
Many gods, many ways to God, many truths that don't bar
Men from doing immoral things and achieving eternal life,
That, in the name of God, fanatically unleash war and strife,
Your religions that teach I evolved from an archangel wholly,
Rebuffing I'm God's Son born from a virgin mother who's holy,
Religions that don't honor my mother ridiculing her power
To intercede for men bringing their pleas to me any hour,
As she will be with me in heaven
Closely, as she was on Earth even
When she pleaded me to help humans
In their time of needs more than once,
Your religions that refute my death, resurrection, and ascension
To heaven to sit on the right hand of God without question,
After my painstaking and resounding accomplishment;
And my inevitable return to Earth for my final judgment.
Your religions that affirm that there is neither heaven nor hell,
That God doesn't punish for sin, and therefore, all will be well,
Your religions that profess hopelessness, by asserting there's no hope
Beyond death, negating my teaching that, after death, life won't stop,
Your religions that isolate me from the Holy Spirit and God the Father,
And glorify only me, even though all of us should be credited together,
Your religions that link my name to pseudo science and unproven
Assertions that only a few thousand souls will make it to heaven,

Whereas I've died willingly so that all believers live with me forever
Because of the work I've done on the cross without human endeavor.

LUCIFER
What's the nature of that particular religion of the last days with which
I can draw all men towards me, making their hearts to burn and to itch?

CHRIST
It's a mishmash or hodgepodge of religions, a sort of cocktail
Mixed by the False Prophet, which all will ecstatically hail
Thinking that a new religion has been found;
But all those that embrace it are hell-bound.

LUCIFER
When will you end my deception with which your teaching I mire?

CHRIST
Your saga shall end when I toss you into the Lake of Fire

(pause)

Man's soul will be a trophy for which you and I will be in fierce contest.
You, to take it to hell to make it suffer; I, to get it to heaven to let it rest.
Whether a human being is a pauper or king, whether he is short or tall,
Well-formed or deformed, prizing his soul, we'll compete for his soul.

Christ pauses realizing that Lucifer has a question.

LUCIFER
If your children are really your children, and indeed, if all
Mine are mine, why do we've to compete for their soul?

CHRIST
My children would forget on Earth they're mine. So that they remember
They're mine, I've to awaken them from their spiritual death or slumber.
Because of sin you'll have them commit, they'll be spiritually dead
Therefore, they'd be unable to decipher the past and what lies ahead.
Besides, you'll be taking mine illegally and legally; and I've to claim
Them back to me legally at the right time. That'll be my long term aim.
I say illegally, because they were supposed to be mine forevermore
They were not meant to ally with you even for a second let alone for
So many years. Regrettably, I'll banish them in the beginning,
For making me a liar, and for listening to your lie and sinning.

Once they side with you, you'll claim them legally,
And take them with my consent and approval, actually.
In the spiritual realm, everything I say has already taken place,
It'll take time before it happens in the material time and space.
Everything we had imagined that has quintessence,
Has already happened in our divine conscience.

LUCIFER
How'll I lose humans after I get them? This is troublesome.

CHRIST
I'll free them paying a dear price to justice as ransom,
As sin involves the breaking of my law, it has consequence.
Either the sinners or someone else should be punished hence.
Lest you grumble saying, I've double standard,
And then, will I be by you unjustly slandered.
I've to reach out for them without delay
In order to expedite their salvation day.
When I gently knock on their heart's door, if they don't open it and race
To let me in, they'll suffer with you, instead of basking in my grace.
The sooner my children join me, even without delaying for a moment,
The sooner they'll be delivered from your jaws and undue torment.

Christ pauses and continues.

In the last days, you'll perform miracles that have never been heard
Of, using the False Christ. Many will follow you like a fearful herd.
You'll aspire to make my good teaching and religion null and void.
The Mystery Babylon Religion will prosper, being hard to avoid.
Your man, the False Christ, will force all to take his name's mark
Without that mark, none will buy or sell. Everything will look dark!
Those who refuse to take the Mark, you'll imprison, enslave, and kill.
Many of my children won't take the Mark, and you'll their blood spill.
European nations will surrender their sovereignty to you under the excuse
Of unity, and give you Europe on a golden plate for your personal use.
While you dwell in the False Christ, Europe will be your launch-pad to take
Over the rest of the world, making it easy for you like eating a piece of cake.
You'll bewitch Europeans with your Babylonian religion and magical power,
And with the charisma of your Fake Christ, who will among them tower.
Euphoric European leaders will pass on their power to him for one hour;
Until I come down to Earth with my terrific angelic army, and shatter
Them all to pieces till their broken bones scatter and their blood splatter.

LUCIFER
How would I perform miracles through
My priests making them look like true?

CHRIST
Being the originator of all sorts of diseases, you'll make men ill,
And when your priests say, "In Christ's name, leave Devil" You will
Leave temporarily. You'll wait for a while, and make them again ill.
For instance, you'll make a person deaf or lame.
When your priests, pastors or evangelists blame
You for it, and command you to leave in my name,
You'll get out, and he will hear or walk with no obstacle.
People will applaud your men for performing a miracle.
This way they'll generate for your church lots of money and members.
What becomes of that person later is irrelevant, and nobody remembers.
Those are the evangelists, apostles and pastors who'll say
To me on that inevitable, long-awaited Judgment Day,
"Didn't I open the eyes of the blind in your name?
"Didn't I raise the dead and cure the lame?"
And I'll say to them, "You children of iniquity,
"I don't know you! Your place is hell for eternity!"

LUCIFER
Well, I must really be a sly imposter; in fact, a formidable factor,
If I can mislead many, using an unsuspecting evangelist or pastor.

CHRIST
Being so unsuspecting that they're obediently serving you, the enemy,
Many pastors, evangelists and apostles would think they're serving me.

Some like to willingly serve you. Woe betide the innocent ones among
These, lest they come speedily to me repenting that they've done wrong!
The members of your congregations too, are surely bound to hell,
If they don't wake up and rush to me when I ring the alarm bell.

(pause)

Among the many religions you'll concoct that hurt me most
Are the ones that bear my name. In them, many will get lost.
Your cunning priests will quote from my books, do your miracles,
Acknowledge my Godhood here and deny it there, and cause debacles
And doctrinal confusions... You'll build edifices that flash with gold,
In which not I, but you dwell, because, in it, your evil religion is sold.

(pause)

Your priests will tell me they honor me, yet dishonor my holy mother,
Whom I've honored and chosen among women, who'll suffer together
With me all my life and during my perilous and arduous ministry,
In whose holy womb I'll dwell for nine months being a mystery,
Whose flesh I'll wear honorably and carry with me for eternity,
In whose flesh I'll dwell among men representing the Trinity.
I, the Holy One, will I ever stay in unholy womb?
Even my dead body won't ever stay in unholy tomb.
My very presence in them makes holy the tomb and womb.

LUCIFER
Your mother? You, the Creator?

CHRIST
You'll understand this later

(pause)

Oh, yes, your pastors will negate that I'll respond to her intercession
When she appears before my throne on behalf of others with compassion.
Let alone my mother who is dear and near to me on Earth and in heaven,
I'll listen and respond when even others pray for their beloved ones, even.
From far away. But why do you say through the mouth of your disciple
Or priest that my mother cannot plead with me to help troubled people?
And you say audaciously that the dead cannot intercede for the living.
Am I the God of the dead? Aren't all those who die in me receiving
Eternal life from me? Isn't being absent from the body being present
With me in heaven? Is my mother who is in heaven with me, absent?
Isn't my mother as alive as I am, even as are all those who've believed
In me? Don't we hear in heaven when men cry from Earth aggrieved?
(pause)

Those who love me ought to adore my mother whom I love and adore.
Because of her, they shouldn't close on themselves their salvation door.

LUCIFER
(shocked and confused)
Who's your mother? When did I say anything against her, Almighty?

CHRIST
You've already spoken against her in eternity.
I hear the echo of your voice and its reverberation,
And I sense distinctly your mind's aberration.

Am I not He who commanded saying, "honor your mother and father"?
So, why wouldn't I honor and obey in everyway my beloved mother?

(pause)

Not every woman wills to endure with me what Mary will endure.
Besides, it's hard to find a woman like her with a heart so pure.
How dare you say my mother is worthless when she agrees to cooperate
With me to save men, sharing my lot when I get distressed and desperate.

As to Mary, my beloved, holy mother, you'll be the cause of much confusion
About her. People will mistake her for "The Queen of Heaven", your fusion
Of my great, holy and divine life history, with the corrupted and coarse
One of yours, as time goes by, and you reach the end of your life's course.
There will be an Ethiopian queen of Egypt called "The Queen of Heaven".
You'll deviate her from the true religion of her Ethiopian ancestors given
To them by King Melchizedek, their forefather, a great human being
Who'll be my high priest, in whose order I will be priest and king.
This Ethiopian queen shall worship you, and she, herself, will
Be worshiped by her Egyptian subjects as god. She will fill
The Egyptian temples with your imposing images and those
Of hers. You'll then be called Amon. That's how the story goes.
Some of my own children will confuse Mary, my mother,
With the Queen of Heaven, and blatantly blame my other
Children who honor and adore her like I, myself, do even;
Accusing them of worshiping her as "The Queen of Heaven",
Because they beseech Mary to bring before my throne their prayers,
Though she has nothing to do with the Queen. Hence, my anger flares.

LUCIFER
(in his heart)
I'm so curious how I'll be called Amon and be worshiped. I can't wait
To attain godhood! How will I convince men I'm god? With what bait?

CHRIST
(hearing his heart)
You'll appear like an angel of light to some religious fanatics
In the image of Gabriel or Michael applying deceptive tactics.
You'll hatch and breed enthralling and intriguing false religions
That contradict or compromise my teachings, in all the regions.
Of the world and in all ages, bearing this and that name.
But when one scrutinizes them, they'll all be the same.

You're safe as long as I'm not in the center of these
Counterfeit religions you'll minister and sell with ease.
You'll distort my truth blending it with your lies intimately,
Propagating all religions lead to the same God ultimately.
However, you and I know that your religion, if you tell
The truth, won't lead anyone to me, but to you and hell.
With some of your religions you'll refute my divinity, my birth
From a virgin, and my being God's Son, when I'm born on Earth.
You'll deny I'm God Almighty, equal to Father God and the Holy
Spirit; divine every inch and in every attribute, and indeed wholly.
When you falsely teach I'm a simple prophet, and a man less than
God, some will believe you, for such a falsehood appeals to man.

LUCIFER
How exactly would my religion be
Different? This is not clear to me.

CHRIST
Your religion will delude many nations declaring that I'm not
God, that I'm only a god among many gods, that there are a lot
Of prophets among which I'm one, that I'm not the first and last,
That I won't descend to Earth in flesh, that I am not the past
Present and future, that I won't be born from a virgin to be light
To all and to save mankind by dying and rising to sit on God's right
Hand, that I won't return to Earth to judge all, and reign being upright,
That I'm not the only truth and the only way, and the only God-given
Savior of men, and that one should not believe in me to go to heaven,
That I'm not the only God men ought to adore and worship,
That there is no punishment for sin, and that sinners can skip
Hell and the Lake of Fire. You'll deny these in your religions of occult
That lead to the Lake of Fire as a result, making the way to me difficult.
Most of all, you'll deceive humans making them believe they will be
Gods or are already, and that they shouldn't worship their Creator, me.

Christ looks towards some of the fallen angels and continues speaking...

All you fallen angels will be so retarded and degenerated
That you'll decay, get insane, filthy, ugly and infuriated
By your miserable conditions. Eventually, all of you will act
Like demons doing untold evil. None of you will remain intact.
Some of you'll change your shape and obtain fake sexual organs,
And play the role of human male and female in order to advance
Your perversion agenda to act as homosexuals and lesbians.
Humans will be homosexuals when you possess humans.

Some of you'll act like male and female homosexuals to team
Up, and have sex with human males and females in a dream,
Imprinting on their spirits strong feelings, as well as extreme
Emotions that affect them when they wake up from their dream.
The homosexual spirits will then implant in them irresistible desire
And urge to have sex with their own sex without a moral quagmire.
Unaware of the spiritual forces behind this activity, to be logical,
Humans will justify it as being social, psychological, and biological.
That I've perfectly created humans as male and female so that they can
Reproduce children, you all know full well. That's how I designed man.

The only way humans could be normal is if I extricate
You out of their lives, and when they hate their state;
And of course, if they come to me and entreat
Me to help them. But if they reject me and retreat
Away from me liking and enjoying their sinful practice,
As much as I love them, I can't help them, as you'll notice
In the years to come. When you beguilingly begin to play
A filthy and unnatural role in human life in every way,
Being consumed by lust after the same sex, to my dismay,
And marrying with the same sex, shall be the order of the day.
Women shall avoid men and conceive without men,
Men will have children without copulating with women.
Thus, women shall raise confused kids without fathers.
And men shall breed messed up babies without mothers.
To me, sexual perversion
Is a tremendous aversion!

You'll act like husbands and wives to humans when they're in deep
Slumber, and engage their spirits in sexual intercourse in their sleep,
Thus making them lose interest in having sex with their spouses;
Causing frigidity, impotence, discord, and divorce in many houses.

Christ addresses Azazel and Semazya.

And you, Azazel and Semazya, I wish I didn't create
You, because, the harm you'll do is horrific and great—
You'll teach humans witchcraft and sorcery bewitching every nation,
So that they'll destroy each other without kindness and compassion.
You'll show them how to shift their human shape to a horse,
Hyena, crocodile, lizard, bird or any animal, without remorse,
To hurt their fellow human beings I've created lovingly in my image.
Instead of coming to me in prayers for help anytime and in every age,

Sadly, many will flock after you, bewitched by your mesmerizing magic.
Consequently, the world will be belligerent, bloody, wicked and tragic.
You'll show women cosmetic, and how to wear make up with dedication;
To seduce men to lust after them, and to commit adultery and fornication.
This, you do, so that the foundation of my moral laws are totally shaken,
And my good commandments by which men should abide are broken.

Christ pauses detecting Azazel wants to say something.

AZAZEL
Will we do so because you spoke thus, or will we commit our crime
Because of our own wickedness and volition at that period of time?

CHRIST
This is prophecy. I'm neither commanding
You, nor am I this from you demanding
In order to hit my target. This'll be your evil lot,
Whether I prophecy all these future events or not.
(after a short pause to Azazel)
Azazel, when you get worst, Michael shall imprison you under the River
Euphrates for a long time, so that you won't hurt men as a sly deceiver.

LUCIFER
Will I, too, be under water or out?

CHRIST
You'll be out,
So that you can accomplish my mission wherever you roam about.
But I'll jail you for one day in hell, to your dismay,
When I reign in my Holy City on Earth for one day,
So that this abused world can from your trouble rest
At least for one day, when I take over and rule best.

LUCIFER
(mumbling)
Your one day is one thousand long human years.
Am I to suffer that long in hell in pain and tears?

GABRIEL
Are you kidding yourself Lucifer…You're getting hilarious.
You know you'll burn in the Lake of Fire forever. Be serious…

CHRIST
(ignoring Lucifer's concern)
After the one thousand years, I'll release you for a short while,
So that you can stir and misguide my enemies with your vile.
I'll make you entice the army of wicked men with mighty power
To attack my Holy City so that I can obliterate them in one hour.
Shortly after, it will be your end. Your time will expire—
You, your men and angels will head to the Lake of Fire.
My children, my angels and I, won't deal with you any longer.
We'll have eternal peace and joy—-Your menace won't linger.
Christ's eyes become tear-dimmed

All of you will defile and demolish man, my sacred edifice,
By demanding of your evil worshippers human sacrifice.
You'll even demand that parents sacrifice their own children, therefore.
You'll thirst for blood and literally drink it demanding more and more.

LUCIFER
How can this be? Will we angels truly be so perverted?
I can't imagine us to be so pernicious and so inverted!

CHIRST
We had known eons ago that you'll be a sad story,
When you were nothing, but a mist in our memory.

(pause)

In your last days, you'll unleash in desperation drugs and violence
That shake and rock the world in a terrific calamity and turbulence.
You'll have your scientists engineer diseases genetically, and infest
My healthy world with incurable illnesses and uncontrollable pest.
You do this vile thing to wipe out my creatures intending to decrease
Earth's populations, so that your evil children can take Earth with ease.
You'll divert away men from me through entertainment and sport,
That will make them lose their minds in frenzy and transport
Them away from my reality, giving them no time to meditate
On and think about me and the purpose of living in such a state.

(pause)

Overall, you're the author of diseases and pain, time and again.
It's not in my nature to make my beings suffer from any pain.

(pause)

When pregnant women give you attention and stray
Away from me, and don't for their protection pray,
You'll cause the birth of retarded and deformed babies,
Wrenching my heart. You'll even madden dogs with rabies.
And then men wonder why I create deficiently, and blame
Me for bringing into the world the retarded, blind, and lame.
Verily, I like to see my humans and animals healthy and glad.
You make them handicapped, sick, crazy, depressed and sad.
You make sick. I heal.
I clothe. You peel.
I build. You demolish.
I make wise. You make foolish.

*Lucifer wonders in his heart why God would allow him to exercise so much freedom.
Christ contemplates in pain for a moment and continues.*

Sadly, you were allowed to do all these mishaps and evil
When you were nebula; long before you became the Devil.
And at that time, we decided to grant all our creatures freewill.
Had we decided otherwise, had we really made your freewill nil,
All of you would've been nothing, but robots driven by our will.
We were in dilemma to create either robotic things,
Or decision-making and free-willed living beings.
Yet, we settled for free-willed living beings,
Instead of inanimate, dull and robotic things.

Christ looks at the good angels lovingly.

Look at our good angels who won't do any ill
Against us and all, abusing their freewill.
We're comforted by them and filled with thrill.
We won't regret that we've granted freewill.

LUCIFER
I still don't get it why you wouldn't hurry to stop my crime?

CHRIST
Rest I assured I will stop your crime at my own time...
Indeed there'll be a time when I, against you take action.
But my delayed time, compared with eternity, is a fraction.

Many will think I've forgotten to return soon.
I promise, I'll return any time, midnight or noon.

I can't leave a job half-done. My return to Earth is eminent.
My delay is temporary, though men think it's permanent. .
I'll give men enough time before my return to prepare
Them for salvation and free themselves from your snare.
They'll make me a liar if they think I won't return. I confirm
That I'll return, for sure. My promise to my children is firm
Everything I'm saying and promising is real, and not an illusion.
Your madness and my plans should reach their logical conclusion.
Nor will I allow this horrendous condition to continue forever.
I've to stop it at one point never to allow it again. Yes, never!

LUCIFER
It seems that man is attracted to me more than
To you. Why'd I draw towards me your man?

CHRIST
I being a Supreme God, Omnipotent, Omniscient and Holy,
Am accessible through holiness, prayers and fasting only.
You are cheap, unholy and easily available and accessible
To those that are unholy, destructive, weak and gullible.
When those that seek me with prayers and patience get
At my throne, I'll help them so that they, their woes forget.
You, however, ensnare them to enslave them, to destroy
Them, make them stray away from me, and steal their joy.
Yet, those whose hearts are pure, or those for whom I've a task,
I'll approach joyfully even if they don't beg me anything or ask.

LUCIFER
To reach my children, what's my medium of communication?

CHRIST
You'll teach them magical rituals and incantation.
And then you will materialize before them vividly
To conspire against Almighty God and man avidly.
You and your angels will maneuver and possess their mind,
Whenever your wicked mind and theirs click and are aligned.
If they reject you and decide to lock you out successfully,
You'll penetrate their heads and possess them forcefully.
You'll control their mind also through radio, motion pictures,
TVs, books, and music reflecting violence, lies and evil features.

LUCIFER
(in his heart)
Of course, I know books, music and evil features;
But what are TVs, radio and motion pictures? ...

CHRIST
(ignoring Lucifer's question)
Since I give men good laws by which to abide and deal
With life, saying, "don't kill, don't lie, and don't steal",
Your lawlessness attracts them when you say, for real,
"It's okay, kill, steal and lie." You're out to wound, kill and steal
I'm there to give life abundantly; to restore, to comfort, and heal.

(pause)

Your worst scheme to captivate men will be witchcraft. This snares
Men. Since they're very curious to find out what their future bears,
You can entrap them easily when you eloquently tell them a mass
Of their past, and predict a future that may or may not come to pass.
Whereas, if my agonized children come to me in prayers and supplications,
And I see what their future has in store or detect its negative implications,
Since it's I who created time, being the past's, present's and future's master,
I'll change its course for my children's sake, to avert an impending disaster.
But you cunningly make up, and foretell a future disastrous path
Compelling men it'll happen, like one plus one is two in math,
They themselves will make it happen and suffer the aftermath.
First, you will tell them a few truthful events of their past to open
Them up. Then when you predict, they'll believe it'll really happen.
Since some of your many predictions may happen indeed,
Your devilish effort to enslave men spiritually will succeed.

LUCIFER
Lord God, I'm really confused. How can I take over
The world you've created? With what exact endeavor?

CHRIST
Your ambition to take over the entire
World is unstoppable. You won't retire
Until you take it. When you think why you can't take it easily,
You'll realize that it's because there are many nations really.
You'll also know that a nation consists of members of a family.
These citizens harbor strong feelings of nationalism for their country.
Being glued together with common land, religion, culture and history.

You'll hate nationalism, and swear to replace it with internationalism.
In order to reach your goal, you'll design socialism and communism
With which you can break to pieces fiery nationalism and allegiance
To one country, flag, government, religion, and culture in compliance.
To rid of these, you'll divide society by class, and wage revolutions,
Upholding communism's banner, and advocating they're the solutions
To injustice, exploitation of man by man, class gaps and inequality.
You'll preach a godless communism to be Paradise of higher quality.
Thus communism will destroy for you faith in God, loyalty
To family, country, flag, and monarchy, since you hate royalty.

When men are stripped of their feelings of belonging to a country,
Be they from the working class, peasantry, or even the gentry,
No matter how much internationalist they become and feel free,
They'll wither away at one point in time, like an uprooted tree.
They'll be maneuvered into believing they're the citizens of the planet,
Not realizing it's you that's fishing their souls with international magnet.
Because they're godless, they'll be lawless violating my commandments:
"Honor your parents, love all, don't kill, and don't lie ever in all moments."

Such a system of godlessness, lawlessness, bloodshed, and anarchy
That replaces old despots with communistic oppressors and hierarchy,
No doubt, is good for you, and will serve you well—
You'll take the whole world and godless men to hell.

Weishaupt, Marx, Lenin, Stalin, and one called Mao in China, all
These and many of your devotees will enable you to reach your goal.
The powerful, hidden men behind them are bonded, and serve you in secret
When you meet them underground, though they seem pious and discrete.
What is amazing is that they'll give you a pet name, "The Illuminator",
"Reflector of light", whereas in truth, you'll be "darkness-disseminator."
Unfortunately, many young people in many nations, not knowing
That these men are bonded to you, will be deceived. Following
Them blindly thinking they're genuine, they'll sacrifice
Their lives for a Satanic cause, besides committing vice.

LUCIFER
Lord God, do I really deserve to possess so much power?

CHRIST
Though I empower you so, and you seem to tower
Over the universe invincibly, your actual power

Is like the power of a wild, galloping horse
That I ride, and whose bridle I hold relaxed, and control, of course.
Verily, you're a horse I'll ride. I'll restrain you when you get coarse,
Puffed up, and attempt vainly to divert from my intended course.
I'll dump you in that Fire, after I use you to reach my goal,
Though you seem to be mighty, in my court is the real ball.

LUCIFER
It must really be a scary sight to see,
Where could this Lake of Fire be?

CHRIST
It's in Auroria, the Sixth Heaven. Go and see it if you've the guts.

LUCIFER
(shrugging, in his heart)
Oh, no!... Thank you... I'm not that nuts...

CHRIST
Not only see it, you'll swim in it... Don't worry...
The time will rush by itself. Don't be in a hurry...

(pause)

What the Lake of Fire is, I think you can tell.
Hell is a bit complex. Let me now explain hell.
Hell is not heaven. It's a grim place under the earth. The difference
Between hell and Earth is huge. If we use earth as a point of reference
And contrast it with hell, it's just like day and night.
But then hell has its own contrast- darkness and light.
Hell has different strata of dungeons. You'll hold in the darker level,
Which's horrific, the souls over whom you'll have full control as devil.
All human beings that walk with me or those that haven't surrendered
To you totally, will be in the lighter part, because, you haven't rendered
Them to be completely sinful. Temporarily, all of them will stay here.
Everyone that dies has to come and be confined to this place of fear
Until someday I die on Earth, come here in my spirit and forcefully snatch
Some from you to take them to Paradise with a victory that has no match.
Between the time I rise from the dead, ascend to heaven, and to Earth return,
Those who worship you and reject me, or are indifferent to me, will learn
A lesson here for rejecting me or for allying with you; till the Judgment Day
When I judge by their works as to who should be forgiven or head right away
To the fiery Lake. The ones that won't be forgiven are those that intentionally
Reject me, worship you as god avowedly, deliberately, and devotionally,

Exercising evil. If the good works of those whose souls you stole by deception
Disguised as an angel of light weighs heavily, I'll pardon them as an exception.
And those who were hindered from believing in me due to circumstance
Beyond them born in a society where my name is outlawed, for instance,
Or if they never have heard of me and my wonderful salvation plan,
I'll judge them justly and fairly by how they treated their fellow man
Led by that unquenchable, ever-bright light of conscience I have
Placed in the fiber of their being when I molded them with love.

I can't condemn at all anyone by what they were not aware of and exposed
To. I can penalize them only if they knew my commandments and opposed
Them consciously and defiantly. I'll examine their hearts and scrutinize
Their motivation thoroughly. It's only after that, I'll my judgment finalize.
The good ones will go neither to the Lake of Fire nor to Paradise indeed.
As my mansions are many, they'll reside there where it suits their deed.
They're lucky because I spare them the Lake of Fire.
They should praise and raise me higher and higher.
As I'm the fairest of judges and a compassionate God beyond measure
I don't rush to send to the Lake of Fire the souls I've created and treasure.
After all, the keys of the Lake of Fire and heaven are in my possession fully.
I can let in or let out through them any souls, despite my decision to lawfully
Grant salvation to humans to be fair to justice
That I myself uphold and volunteer to practice.
I won't forgive only those who worship you and renounce me in compliance
With you, and those who hear my word repeatedly and reject it in defiance.

In conclusion, hell's like a jail where suspects are confined until judgment.
The Lake of Fire is like prison where they'll serve their final punishment.
Though it was for you, reprehensible angels, I made the Lake of Fire prior
To my fashioning man, ironically, the first to go into the Lake of Fire
Will be your False Christ and his fake prophet, after fulfilling my desire.
Rest assured—All of you will join them later inevitably in the Lake of Fire

The fallen angels look terrified.

LUCIFER
(in his heart)
I wish God will melt and dissolve me away in that unquenchable fire finally,
So that I sense and feel nothing, as I don't want to burn and suffer eternally.

CHRIST
(continuing)
Regarding beautiful Paradise, it's not really the ultimate dwelling of my elect.
They'll be in Aryam, the Fifth Heaven, where my glory will blazingly reflect.

(pause)

In a sophisticated imitation of our Godhood as one and three,
You'll daringly pose as being one and also three, being free
To deceive and confuse men and compete with us in divinity,
By spreading and circulating around the concept of unity,
Organic unity, within plurality. You'll be reverently worshiped
In different countries as Trinity with different names, gripped
With futile ambition to be God. Thus, in India you'll call
Yourself Brahma, Vishnu and Siva. But this is not all.
In Greece, you'll be Zeus, Poseidon and Adonis; in Egypt—Amun or Amon,
Re and Ptah; and in Phoenicia—Ulomus, Ulosuros, as well as Eliun. On
Top of this, in Rome—Jupiter, Neptune and Pluto; in the Germanic Nations—
Wodan, Thor and Fricco; and in Sumeria—Anu, Enlil, and Ea. Your deceptions
Are limitless. You'll also make up ahead of me a story concerning my actual
Birth from a virgin mother by negating the fact that it's exceptional or unusual.
This, you'll do by creating similar myths in countries like Egypt and India about
Osiris, Isis, Set, Nepthys, Horus and Krishna, drawing exact parallel throughout
Your lies concerning my birth, deeds, life and death to saw the seeds of doubt
Concerning my specialty as God of gods, and to contend that my miraculous
Birth and life were not new as they had happened to other gods. It's ridiculous.
Yet, millions will believe it and worship you as Horus, Vishnu, and Krishna, as
Well as many other gods. We created men so that they worship only us.
Fools accept myths for real. They'll succumb to your myths without critical
Thinking. They'd scorn you if they examine your myths, being analytical.
Tragically, you'll turn countless people all over the world away from my light,
Immersing them in the abyss of your darkness until I shine blindingly bright.
Your vain efforts to eclipse me are uncountable.
Yet, I'll outshine you pursuant to my timetable.

(pause)

Now I'll take you into the future, into the 21st Century.
You're there now. Let's talk about your past history.

Lucifer finds himself in the 21st Century. He is amazed at his own appearance, which is far different than his present stature and demeanor.

CHRIST
(watching Lucifer in the 21st Century)
In order to hear the answers from the mouth of the horse.
I'll ask you some questions. I know the answers, of course.
Tell me now in a few words what you, in the days gone-by, told
The Egyptians, Babylonians, Indians and other nations of old

When you were viciously bent to ruin the prophecy
Of my birth from a virgin to save mankind with mercy.

ANGLE ON LUCIFER

LUCIFER
Long before you were born, I made up the story of a mother and son with
Which I could deceive men, called Isis and Horus. According to my myth,
Isis, who is a virgin, mothers Horus by a god called Osiris, himself born
From a virgin. Horus appeared to save the world, which was bad and forlorn.
All three were figments of my imagination. People bought into this fantasy,
And started worshipping me by sacrificing to their sculptures in ecstasy.
Dwelling in their statues invisibly, I compelled men to prostrate at my feet.
I demanded human sacrifice often. I had high priests with their own fleet.

ANGLE ON THE STATUES OF HORUS AND ISIS.

*He points at the idols of Horus and Isis. Isis is about to breastfeed or has already breastfed
Horus. The idol seems like the Madonna, the mother of Jesus Christ carrying her baby Child.*

These are son and mother. They're counterfeit of you, and Mary, your mother.
I counterfeited and duplicated you in India, China, Babylon, and many other
Parts of the world fancying different myths such as that of Krishna. Mary,
Your mother's name, I gave to some of my mothers. When on a missionary
Service some of your Christians went to Asia, they were shocked and scared
By the pagan sculptors made prior to your birth. The men for whom they cared
Posed questions concerning the striking similarities between your mother,
Yourself, and my fake mothers and sons. As a result, some wouldn't go thither.

CHRIST
So you've successfully imitated my mother and myself ahead of my birth with
Counterfeit statutes and pictures in many countries by circulating your myth.

LUCIFER
No question about that. Humans love legends and fairy
Tales. I wanted them to have their own Jesus and Mary
Even in this advanced 21st Century in which there's friction
Between science and religion, people love to buy into fiction.
For the past 2000 years, I admit, I've relentlessly polished and sharpened
My virgin birth story to match yours, as I know now what has happened.

Lucifer holds a US Dollar note in his hand and shows it to Christ.

ANGLE ON A US DOLLAR BILL

Speaking of Horus, here's his All Seeing Eye on a pyramid of a US Dollar bill.

CHRIST
(just to hear what Lucifer has to say)
Why did you do this ill?

LUCIFER
I'm Horus. You've allowed me to own this world. This Dollar bill
Is mine. So, my children put my eye on the bill expressing my will.
I'm sending a message to and warning humans, that though I'm invisible,
I see through everything, since, for me, there's nothing which's not feasible.

CHRIST
You're lying; aren't you? Is it you or I,
Who, in truth, has an "all seeing eye"?

LUCIFER
You know it's you, God Almighty. I can't see beyond the ground
On which I stand. But the world thinks my vision has no bound.

(pause)

I chose to put my eye on top of this unfinished pyramid in order to remind
Myself and my children of our unfinished job. There's a meaning behind
It. The unfinished job is the complete take over of the world in a short while.
Oh, the time is ripe and sweet for us, but for your children—bitter like bile.
When I was Horus in Egypt, I built this Pyramid with the help of the learned
Aliens from planet Memrose, your brilliant beings I've led astray and turned
Evil. The Pyramid used to be my abode where my priests and the populace
Worshipped me. Most of the Pharaohs were Ethiopians. They revered my place
In their lives. I pretended to be their guardian. They served me with devotion.
The pyramids charged me, and I unleashed my witchcraft with commotion.
Those ancient aliens because of whom you sank the old world under water
Are here again. My children and I will use them to advance our cause later.

CHRIST
You bet. This is a serious and truthful matter.
However, you'll use them sooner than later.
And they'll be an unforgettable sign for my arrival
As in the time of Noah when they were my rival.

LUCIFER
On this Dollar bill, I proclaim the advent of my New World Order about
Which I've been dreaming for the past 5000 years. I'm aggressively out

To launch it big time. My program is crystal-clear.
I'm decreeing it to all those who are willing to hear.
Though my program is speaking loudly on the Dollar bill,
The ignorant masses use it only for buying and selling, to fill
Their stomachs, to spend it on entertainment, and to pay a bill.
They don't realize that they're already under my system, which's ill.
My world government will take all of them by surprise. Yes, it's eminent,
As you've allowed me to have it, regardless of the fact it isn't permanent.
I now own banks and businesses. I'm no poor as in the beginning.
I aspire to take all the natural resources of the world. I'm cunning.
I've put everything in place. I look forward for a new adventure.
My New Order isn't about material gain. It's out souls to capture.

CHRIST
If the so-called "all seeing eye" represents you and your nefarious will,
Why is there a caption: "in God we trust" on the very same Dollar bill?

LUCIFER
Why wouldn't there be? They didn't specify which god is behind
The bill. I'm that god. Rest assured—- They didn't have you in mind.

CHRIST
Why don't you focus on the good, old world, instead of the new world?
Remember, in the days gone by she used to be charmingly pearled?

LUCIFER
She's no more as beautiful to me as she used
To be. She's now outdated, outworn and bruised.
The USA replaced the old world. She's the New Atlantis. My servant
Francis Bacon envisioned her when she was yet unknown and vacant,
Populated only by a handful of Indians. He was my initiate. He had a ton
Of information on Atlantis available to the initiate, but not to the simpleton.
As you recall, dear God, Atlantis had reached the climax of her civilization
Far better than the 21st Century. I made her sin against you. Your realization
Of her sin outraged you, even though I was the one who pushed her to commit
So much iniquity. Consequently, you sank her under water forever to omit
Her from your memory and delete her from the map
Of the Earth. In fact, I'm still to blame for her mishap.
A while before you sank her, some of her farsighted dwellers had taken a terrific
Amount of her relics and literature on her scientific achievements with specific
Explanations of spaceships, motion pictures, technology, and agriculture;
In a word, many objects and documents that represented her rich culture.
They placed these things in the hands of my priests in a pyramid
In Egypt for thousands of years. They were kept and examined amid

My initiates. The brightest of them like Francis Bacon gained
Access to them later. This phenomenal English man obtained
A secret knowledge and information on Atlantis more than
Anybody in England... Really, he was not an ordinary man.
He was the best mind of Europe in his time. So, he wrote a tale
Titled "The New Atlantis" in which he reflected with precise detail
Some aspects of the civilization of Atlantis. He played a leading role
In establishing colonies in America to replace under British control
The lost Atlantis with the New Atlantis. Thus, with his tale, he inspired
His fellow Rosicrucians to make America the New Atlantis as he aspired.
People mistakenly think that it was only your Christian Pilgrim
Fathers that established the United States. This makes me grim.

CHRIST
I know the main actors were your initiates; not my Pilgrim
Fathers. Since I know everything, you don't have to be grim.

(pause)
Yet, you've to admit that it's from this great nation and people
That my great missionaries spread the light of my good Gospel
To the darker realms of the world, setting extraordinary example.

LUCIFER
Remember it's also from this same nation full of many an opportunity
My false religions originated, including those that negate your divinity;
And those that teach that you are or evolved from Archangel Michael,
Denying that you're the one that created angels performing a miracle.

CHIRST
Still, the wonderful works of my true believers outweighs,
The evil deeds of your misguided followers, in many ways.

(pause)

LUCIFER
It was my initiates like Francis Bacon and his followers who played
A key role when the corner-stone of the United States was being laid.
I had a strong vision to make America, my New Atlantis, instrumental
In my effort to embark my New World Order. I prepared the mental
State of my initiates to accept my visionary view that transcended time.
Francis Bacon inspired many men for me, because my vision was sublime.
Among those he inspired in the formation of America are Benjamin Franklin
And Thomas Jefferson, who were both my initiates. With a great discipline
They worked to resurrect the old Atlantis and make America the New
Atlantic. Francis Bacon, as you know, was a very brilliant man. He knew

Much about science and literature. In fact he was the greatest playwright
That has ever lived. He used the pen name Shakespeare to avoid a fight
With the royalty of England because of his critical plays, which showed
Them negatively. I spoke to him as the goddess Athena and he vowed
To serve me. I told him with a feminine voice, holding a spear in the form
Of the Greek goddess Athena, that he should write plays that'd transform
The English people into master-colonizers of the world. I impressed
Him and inspired him to write all those plays. Athena bears a spear
In her hand and shakes it against the eye of ignorance without fear.

*Lucifer shows the stature of the Greek goddess Athena wearing a magical helmet
and bearing a spear.*

Athena wears a magical helmet and holds a spear if you look at her at a glance.
According to a myth I fabricated, she shakes her spear at the eyes of ignorance.
In reality, I was Athena disguised as a female goddess. Hence his pen name,
Shake-spear. The actor that was supposed to be Shakespeare was a game
Bacon was playing on the royalty. He was an illiterate who couldn't sign
Even his name properly, let alone compose such plays that were so fine.
It's regrettable that he didn't use his talent to praise you even though you
Endowed him with enormous talent and a bright mind through and through.
As my servant Francis Bacon and I planned, the British not only colonized
America, but the whole world .They were glorified much and even lionized.
It was said of their colony, "the sun never sets in the British Empire". Formally
The USA is independent of Britain. Yet, she is very strongly tied to her actually.

(pause)

O, Lord God, I don't know why I'm telling you
All this. You know everything better than I do

CHRIST
Lucifer, I know everything you're telling me, of course.
Remember I wanted to hear it from the mouth of the horse?
(pause)

What you say about the US, is only something your wishful heart states.
I haven't permitted you to do whatever you like with the United Sates.

LUCIFER
Well, I have to aspire and state my heart's wish,
Even if it won't happen or is absolutely rubbish.

CHRIST
Even though your wish is without bound,
I won't allow you to mess everything around.

(pause)

Your servant, Bacon, how often do you torture
In hell, for serving you devotedly in his literature,
For advancing your wicked adventure,
And for promoting your ill venture?

LUCIFER
I torture him whenever he forgets to praise me in a sonnet.
Oh!... His sonnets enchant and attract my soul like a magnet!
It's ridiculous—-You gave him a rare talent and a brilliant head.
So that he may glorify and praise you. He glorifies me, instead.

(pause)

Francis Bacon not only knew you well, but edited the King James version
Of the English Bible. Yet, he chose to ally with me in a bitter aversion
To your word. Isn't that amazing? Knowing God's word well is not enough.
While I'm lurking around, for humans to love and worship God is tough.

CHRIST
It's not only you that deceived and sadly destroyed him. If you reckon
His situation, it's unquenchable thirst for science that beguiled Bacon.
When men love anything more than God, their Maker, one can easily tell
That the thing will drive them away from their God and lead them to hell.

LUCIFER
That's exactly what I do to humans. I make them focus on life's banality
Instead of you and eternity; to choke them and steal their soul in actuality.
I wonder though, how Bacon would be and write
If I didn't exist. Maybe his writings would be trite.

CHRIST
He'd not have written anything hadn't you existed. All those characters listed
In his plays, as well as the settings, plots and climaxes, wouldn't have existed.
If you didn't exist, there would be no hate, jealousy, betrayal, maniacal ego,
Conspiracy, murder, Brutus, Hamlet, Gertrude, Macbeth, Othello, and Iago.

LUCIFER
(proud of himself)
I, and not Shakespeare, or to be precise, Bacon, should be credited
For all these amazingly perfect plays and sonnets that can't be edited.

(pause)

The house in Stratford-Upon-Avon, that the English display,
As you know, is of the actor, and not of the writer of play.
Have you seen that house paying attention,
Which's now a huge tourist attraction?

CHRIST
I'm watching it paying attention right
Now as we speak. It's an interesting sight.

LUCIFER
It's a deception
Beyond description...
Bacon regrets now that the moron actor took all the honor and fame
Due to him, because he didn't reveal to the world his real, given name.

(pause)

CHRIST
Don't insult the actor for saving Bacon's face. Bacon had him tagged
Up so that he'd, instead of him, be questioned, harassed and nagged.

(pause)

LUCIFER
I'm proud that without me, there wouldn't have been Bacon's, Balzac's, Dante's
Homer's, Virgil's, Goethe's, Milton's, Dostoyevsky's, Tolstoy's and Cervantes'
Writings and characters. I am the author of these authors and their works.
I deserve a Nobel Prize for literature, or at least the highest literary marks.

(pause)

My latest servant-writer to whom my poets should compose an ode
Is one called Dan Brown, author of the novel, *Da Vinci's Code.*
He wrote pure, white lies about you and Mary Magdalene. He's a crook.
My children and I sanctioned, financed and urged him to write this book.
He made all the monies in the world. He achieved instant fame.
Ha! ha! ha!... He'll regret it when he burns with me in that flame!

We promoted the book.. We made it a best-seller and very great.
People bought it fast thinking it cracked a Roman Catholic secret.
But it didn't crack anything really, but the head of the fool—-
The uncritical, the naïve and the one that didn't go to school.

CHRIST
What lies did Dan Brown write about me and Mary, my daughter?

LUCIFER
That she had mothered children by you and settled in France thereafter,
And that the Merovingian kings of France descended from your bloodline.

(pause)

Even I, the liar, attest this is not true, and to tell the truth, I won't decline.

CHRIST
Then why did you and your children slander and defame
Me and my daughter Mary, whose name is a holy name?

LUCIFER
To attack the Roman Catholic Church and lend legitimacy in advance
To my fake Christ, if we wish to link him to you and kings of France.

CHRIST
I heard you saying it long ago before it went out of your mouth and the pen
Of your lair. Even Mary Magdalene was very sad when I told her this, then.
Your so-called writer and you shall pay a dear price for this vilification
When, on my day of wrath, I cast you in the Lake of Fire in vindication.

LUCIFER
I know I've hurt you;
But I had to do what I had to do.

CHRIST
In any case, how's your fake and wicked Christ doing currently?
Check him out and tell me. I'll bet he's being looked upon reverently.

LUCIFER
Your usurper counterpart, my fake Christ, is worshipped in darker regions
By my children clad in mantles of authority. They're leaders of religions
And great nations that claim to be Christians nominally and formally.
Since I'm in him, it's me they worship actually, casually and normally.
He's indescribably charismatic. He charms significant world rulers.
Some of them doubt whether he is really you, but he clouds and blurs

Their vision. Soon they'll irrevocably surrender their power to him,
So that he can trample over them and exercise his insatiable whim.
I will declare him soon in the media. He will bewitch the whole
World speaking in all languages promising a new era. .He'll haul
Everyone towards him. Then, it will be me, who'll be adored by all.

(pause)

I'll be jealous when humans worship my false Christ, as I won't be seen.
I wish I had a human body so that they'll worship me without go-between.

CHRIST

I knew that you wished you were human,
When you first saw me designing man.
You're jealous that I made him above you and love
Him more. You've to accept that he's high above.
After you fell from grace, you went even lower.
You're now the lowest of all. Even animals tower
Higher above you. Had we first created you lovingly in our image
With a human body, you'd have inflicted on man even more damage.
That some humans prostrate to you without any reserve
Is, for you, a big honor you don't whatsoever deserve.
Whoever honors you dishonors himself and us. It's a huge outrage!
It was so that they worship only us we fashioned men in our image.

LUCIFER
(to himself)
First thing first—my man should first be accepted by the rich and poor.

.

CHRIST
How'll you get the whole world to accept your
False Man. What's your recipe to make that sure?

LUCIFER
Oh, that's simple as eating a piece of apple-pie or ice-cream.
We'll operate smoothly and quietly. No need to be loud or scream.
I'll shift his shape occasionally and project his image to portray the appearance
Of the Messiah for the Jews, of Jesus for Christians; assuring their deliverance.
And to the Buddhists he'll fake it as Buddha, which is a huge lie;
And to the Muslims of the world, as Al Mahdi or Al Mahdi's ally.
And to all the adherents of the different religions in the world's different
Nations, he'll appear as the savior they've been waiting for, being patient
For hundreds of years. Thus all will embrace him without suspecting
That my fake man is not the Messiah or Savior they've been expecting.

Of course the magical miracles I'll perform through him will bewitch
The entire world so that they will not notice when I shift and switch
His shape for different occasions and audiences. We'll certainly back
Up his physical appearances with wonders, and all will be taken aback. .

CHRIST
You've planned it out well... So now, they call you Adonai?

LUCIFER
(rocking with laughter)
Yes, they do! Oh, my!... Oh, my!...
They call you "the Devil", and call me "Adonai"!
What a scandal! What a shame! What an incredible shame!
I made them lose their mind and they gave me your holy name!

CHRIST
And where will your spiritual base be?
Look at it right now and tell me.

Lucifer gazes far.

LUCIFER
The city built by twins upon seven hills,
The tiny city within a city of spiritual ills.
It was meant to be your spiritual base.
I defiled her by infiltrating her, phase.
By phase, step by step, until I became her heart.
What's left of yours at present is just a little part.
That blessed city, blessed from my perspective,
In which I fed your followers to lions, irrespective
Of their age, thus showcasing my power, so that their blood would flow
Longer than River Rubicon, but deeper than it though it seemed shallow.
And how could it be your base when it was founded by brothers raised
By a she-wolf? No wonder her dwellers acted like wolf and were crazed.
They shamefully watched as one watches game sports, while the wild
Lions tore your children apart, their blood flowed, and their bones piled.

CHRIST
How about your computer; your evil computer
With which you'll human beings monitor?

LUCIFER
My computer called the "Great Beast" is ready.
My surveillance cameras are everywhere steady.

129

My motion pictures, televisions, radios, papers, all
My media and music are thriving under my control.
My armies, banks, priests, sorcerers, and henchmen are well prepared.
My high ranking servants in Europe and the US are all set, and paired.
Many of the things you prophesied about me have come to pass;
And the rest are likely to happen. They serve me like a compass
By which I'm guided. Behold, I've managed to pervert
Some of your beings successfully. I've been able to convert
Them into anything I wanted. They've no moral and feelings of shame.
Not only they're homosexuals and lesbians, but also marry with the same
Sex. Mind you, among them are professionals—lawyers, scholars, artists,
Intellectuals, doctors, engineers, statesmen, businessmen and even priests.
Your sacred marriage between a man and a woman is defiled in this age
Using my sweet judges and lawmakers, I've legalized same sex marriage.

(pause)

Speaking of banks, we've made Switzerland a safe haven for theft,
The Swiss banks hide in plain view illicit riches from right and left.
All the dictators and despots of the world steal the national wealth
Of the countries they lead and stash them in a sophisticated stealth
With secret code numbers only they know, hoping to enjoy it someday
When their people rise up in rage to crush them, and in panic flee away.
Funny enough, most of these thieves die before they escape to enjoy
The stolen silver and gold; and my children confiscate them with joy.
When Hitler "holocausted" your people, my children put their hand
On your people's possessions and stored them in our Switzerland.
For this reason, we didn't allow Switzerland to get involved in the last
Two world wars. But we can't guarantee she'll survive next war's blast.
We'll try our best to protect Switzerland from melting or burning to ash,
So that our stolen riches won't burn to ash or be with molten liquid awash.

(pause)

CHRIST
Woe betide that corrupt nation that welcomes and receives
Bloody silver and gold, and serves as a den of thieves!

(pause)

How's Hollywood, your film industry, doing at the moment,
Are you very pleased that it's extremely bloody and violent?

LUCIFER
(excited)
Oh, yeah! That's my evil headquarter, my remote control
By which, from a distance, I direct the mind and soul of all.
Look at all the brutal violence and curse I unleash and the evil messages
I send through my perverted movies to viewers of the world of all ages.
Look at my Hollywood, that should actually be called "cursed-wood".
All the best actors and performers are mine. I raise them to star-hood
Overnight as soon as they vow to serve me. How? I do nothing unusual
To achieve this. My children own the media, both the audio and visual.
In exchange for their souls, I offer them money and instant fame.
I make them pay a price if they backslide after I elevate their name.
As long as they're in contract with me, they're all obliged to glorify me.
Yes, they've to adore and worship me as their god whoever they may be.

(pause)

I've also tossed your Ten Commandments out of the courts and the schools.
Your Commandments," don't kill, don't lie, and don't steal" were cardinal rules
By which men have withstood my temptations for the past three thousand odd
Years. They've minimized my vices, and made human beings think about God.
Without them, youngsters are completely lost like a ship without a captain.
As a result, lying, killing, and stealing are now rampant and hard to contain.
This exhilarates me! Hail to my judges that I've placed in the hierarchy!
Without them, I wouldn't have been able to unleash killings and anarchy.

(pause)

I'm proud of myself! Hurrah! I'm a hero in every Occidental town.
I'm revered also in the Orient. I've turned your plans upside down!
Oh, I'm a gallant! I deserve to wear a garland and a diamond crown!

CHRIST
(with a tone of anger)
Halt!... Don't get carried away!
Sooner or later I'll have it my way!

Lucifer coils and retreats.

LUCIFER
Sorry... indeed, I got carried away...

CHRIST
Is the situation ripe for your next big war, which, for you, is dear?

LUCIFER
(with a calm voice)
Oh, I'm so excited about it! It is drawing near!
That old, eternal conflict between the stupid Arabs and Jews
Has reached its climax. For me, it's sweeter than mango juice.
Now everything is in place, absolutely without illusion.
All I need is the last world war to reach my conclusion.
There are ethnic conflicts every where. For men, these are dog days of pain!
There are rumors of war. The naive longs for peace and tranquility in vain.
I need a Third World War to wrap up the world under one government,
The next war will enable me to steal all souls. I see this by discernment.
I'll have a world I will lead recklessly with my fake Christ,
Surely, I know I can't attain this unless the situation is worst.
To push everything that's out of control from bad to worst and worse,
I need terribly this next major world war; and not useless small wars.
To achieve this, I've to play it smart.

CHRIST
Where do you want your next world war to start?

LUCIFER
I'm convinced the best place to start it is in the Middle East
Between the Arabs and Jews, so that they'll fight like a beast.
After that, I'll expand it rapidly and make
It between Muslims and Christians to take
All by surprise. Then I'll involve Europe, Russia and her allies—- Persia,
Egypt, Ethiopia, Libya, Syria, all Arabs, and the entire continent of Asia.
My children and I will leap up with joy when the senseless war rages.
And after all the fools obliterate each other, we'll dance on their carnages
This way, we will take the world with ease,
Then, everything will be far better than it is. .

(pause)

My visionary children and I have waged two tragic world wars in the past
To profit much from these wars, and to form a world government that'd last.
We gained a lot financially, but they didn't deliver a world government.
This next war will do it and bring a lasting peace, which's an achievement.
The next world war is only about fishing souls I desperately want in hell,
In order to jam hell, I've to launch it soon. It's time to ring the war-bell.
The plan of my children is to reduce the population of the world to only
500 million out of six billion. I don't care a bit if all humans perish vainly.
Some of my children are concerned that Earth is too crowded to feed
Six billion people. They're playing God in thinking so. It's sheer greed

That makes billions to starve. If Earth's wealth is distributed
Evenly, all will be fed and housed. My children have contributed
Beyond measure, to the world's unbearable, shocking and critical
Condition. Yet, they feign to be its savior. To me, it's hypocritical.
If they share the wealth they've amassed denying humanity access
To prosperity, existence wouldn't be a failure. It would be success.

CHRIST
Since you don't give a hoot for the poor, when you're being critical
Of your own children, aren't you too, being funnily hypocritical?

LUCIFER
You know I've been grotesquely hypocritical
Ever since I rose against you, being critical.

CHRIST
I also heard you speak about bringing peace. Aren't you joking?
Is it you or me, who, in truth, is peace's Lord, Prince, and King?

LUCIFER
You know full well that I'm peace's obstruction
And the prince of war, chaos and utter destruction.
My children kid themselves saying they'll bring peace and reconciliation,
After they deface Earth and obliterate her inhabitants, in mad jubilation.

CHRIST
Wouldn't your children too, be immensely affected?
If, out of six billion, only 500 million are expected
To live, how would they by themselves thrive,
And how do they know whether they'll survive?

LUCIFER
They're crazy. Of course, they're not immune to nuclear attack.
They depend on their secret bunkers that are likely to crack.
Whether humans will survive this terrific nuclear war, I doubt.
In all candor, I don't care a scintilla if this war totally wipes out
All. All I care for is destruction, carnage, and blood
I can drink when it gushes out and flows like a flood.

CHRIST
You mean you don't care even if your children are annihilated
After they've served you so long, being obedient and humiliated?

LUCIFER
Care for men? You know I don't give a damn for your creatures...
Please excuse my French. Hate and destruction are my features.

CHRIST
Aren't your children worried at all that this might cause their pain?
What if it backfires? What if they lose, when they gamble to gain?

LUCIFER
They've stopped thinking ever since they met me for the first time.
I've been doing their thinking for them ever since that time. I climb
Above their shoulders and sit on their heads, and sternly give orders
That they carry out without ifs and buts, like soldiers and warders.

CHRIST
It's not as simple as you put it. You deal with sophisticated and intelligent
Persons that lead nations and institutions. They're most capable and diligent.

LUCIFER
Certainly! I don't waste my brief time on Earth with a bunch of fools.
Yet, no matter how powerful and bright they may be, they're my tools.
Some are naïve and think they can change the world. Most are as vicious
As I am, if not worst. All of them hate you. They're wicked and capricious.

CHRIST
But you hate them too;
Don't you?

LUCIFER
I hate them till I'm blue!
Why should I love them; I'm not you!

CHRIST
But you do love their money, and use their mind, fame and power
To dismantle the world ruthlessly and pluck human life like flower.

(pause)

Speaking of money, soon, suddenly, you'll abolish coins and bank notes
To form that last cashless system, even for both the haves and have-nots.

LUCIFER
This'll be the apex or climax of my success
That'll enable me to control all. When I asses

My prospect looking and analyzing everything from my perspective,
It's very bright, granted it's your permission that makes it effective.

CHRIST
Yes, do what I've assigned you to do. As you
Do your part, I'll do mine, when my time is due.
Tell your nutty children in higher places who possess power and things,
That I won't allow them to annihilate billions of my innocent beings.
Say this to them, "I promise I'll sweep away yourselves, and scatter like dust
"Your carcasses. I'll exterminate you out of existence eternally. My disgust
"And rage will make you burst into pieces and dissolve you with my insistence.
"Thus said Lord of Lords, Almighty God that spoke the universe into existence."

LUCIFER
I will...As for me, if you were not delaying me, I'm ready, willing and able.

CHRIST
How many times do I've to tell you about my timetable?

LUCIFER
I don't know why I'm rushing to that awful, fiery lake. I'm like a snowflake
That longs for a heat that'll melt it. I've to act slowly, lest soon, I face the lake.

(pause)

Lucifer gets excited all of a sudden and leaps up.

CHRIST
Why are you suddenly elated?

LUCIFER
Though my children and I are hated,
We're sophisticated,
And complicated.
My brilliant scientists are working frantically,
To engineer and perfect a deadly virus genetically,
So that we can wipe out a third of mankind, particularly
Blacks, whom my children deem sub-human regularly.
Soon I can dance and sing saying, "trily tralala! trily tralal!
"My scientists have invented a deadly disease called Ebola!"
Ebola will do the job... Oh, yes, it'll shake and rock
The planet... Compared with Ebola, AIDS is a joke.

We manufactured AIDS virus in the laboratory. However, its effect
Was not as devastating as we had expected. It was not perfect.
My children will profit twice from Ebola as they've patented the medicine--
They'll eliminate the unwanted and gain much from the sale of its vaccine.
Moreover, when particularly those Africans are eliminated,
We'll take their minerals and natural resources, unabated.
And when we succeed with Ebola,
We'll celebrate it as an event of gala!
We'll also guzzle whisky with cola,
For our achievement with Ebola!

CHRIST
Dream on! Be elated like you've never been,
Whether this happens remains to be seen...
Verily, verily, you and your nefarious children will pay
For all this, a heavy price, when I judge you someday!

LUCIFER
Indeed, someday we'll face your judgment.
But right now, we will enjoy the moment...

(pause)

CHRIST
How about the Muslim militant
Fighters. Aren't they important?

LUCIFER
Oh, they're very important. I love particularly
The Jihadist radicals who battle regularly.
My children and I need them very badly.
They're sparks that can ignite a major war madly.
We need them to continuously charge the atmosphere
Until the Third World War is launched by me, Lucifer.
For now, I'll have a bit of blood here and there, a bit high, a bit low,
And when you add up the bits, it will indeed be a substantial flow.

We'll use the terrorists as a bogyman or a scarecrow with which to scare
The masses and snatch away their freedom promising them to take care
Of the terrorists for them. At the same time, we'll secretly arm and strive
To train and finance the terrorists so that they can keep their fire alive.
We'll provoke the terrorists; and when they attack the people,
We'll insanely mobilize our army against them. It's that simple.

Those who aren't actually with you are with me by default;
Whether it's their fault that they reject you, or not their fault.
Jihadists practice violence. Love and nonviolence are what you teach.
Jihadists force men to believe in their religion. But you kindly preach.
You knock on the heart's door gently. I don't like your freewill approach.
I love the Jihadists' violence. It's close to my heart. But this, you reproach.

CHRIST
This is a moment of truth—- What's your ultimate mission, and exact desire?

LUCIFER
I'm out to steal souls to burn with me in the Lake of Fire.
After what's said and done, this is my mission and desire.
It's a mission of destruction,
Backed up by nefarious action.

CHRIST
What'll you gain if your children and all men burn with you in the Fire?

LUCIFER
Nothing. Burning alone is something I dread and don't want.
Now that I've worshipers, my chance of burning alone is scant.

CHRIST
And what precisely do your children want?

LUCIFER
They want from me freedom to sin, magical power, sex, money and fame.
I'll give them all these; but their end is tragic—-it isn't nonzero sum game.
In addition, my far-sighted children desire to conquer the world ultimately
Under my leadership on top of the hierarchy. All of us will work intimately
To attain this. All have money up to their teeth. Their mission
This time around is nobler than money. They have a big vision,
A final vision. They want to transform the whole world terminally
With my one world religion practiced physically and subliminally.
Your religion and your believers are our obstacle and adversary.
To get them out of our way, liquidating them soon is necessary.

CHRIST
How did your avaricious children benefit financially
From the past two world wars, at their end and initially?

LUCIFER
Initially, we lent money secretly to all the belligerent nations
At the end of the wars, we lent them again for reconstructions.
This way we craftily compounded and multiplied our booty gain,
Regardless of the fact that the wars had caused unbearable pain.
My children financed and pushed Hitler to invade Europe,
So that they could loan money to all the fighters in the scope
Of the horrendous wars and amass incalculable profit.
Indeed, the wars fetched my children a lot of benefit.

(pause)

Ha! ha! ha!... I remember how we tricked that midget, Napoleon Bonaparte.
We enticed him to invade Europe and financed him and those who took part
Against his war. When he found out that my shrewd children have lent
Money both to France and Britain, he was mad at them and hell-bent
On wiping them out from the surface of the Earth. By the way,
That midget was my initiate in my French secret society. He lay
Flat before my feet in recognition of my authority, as did Alexander,
That Macedonian war-monger. Both men prostrated to me being under
My authority. But the common men that prostrated to them didn't know
They were my servants, and that it was me who raised them from below.
Yet, reflecting in retrospect, both of them have tried their best to take over
The entire world for me, even though they failed in their bold endeavor.
Their attempt was aborted because it was premature. Even Hitler's brazen
Aggression to revive the Roman Empire was thwarted for the same reason.
But my False Christ will conquer for me the whole world in the right season.

CHRIST
How many of the leaders of the world have stooped down to you so far
In your adventurous journey on Earth calling yourself a "morning star."?

LUCIFER
All kings, queens presidents and prime ministers, who've been significant
Have knelt down before me and kissed my feet in self-humiliation. Scant
Are world leaders that didn't prostrate to me and worship me in submission,
Except Ethiopian kings whose forefather, Ethiop, had gone on a mission
To Ethiopia from Jerusalem sent by you to live there, so that, at your birth,
His descendants would bring you gold, myrrh, and incense, best gifts of Earth.

CHRIST
Why do you think those Ethiopian emperors
And kings didn't bow down to you like others?

138

LUCIFER
They were descendants of Melchizedek, on whose order you'll become
King and High Priest in Jerusalem for a millennium, in the years to come.

CHRIST
That's right. It was because, they too, were high priests and kings in the order
Of their forefather, Melchizedek, King of Salem, that they didn't surrender
To you. They loved me and worshiped only me. They weren't pernicious.
When I was born in Bethlehem, they brought me gifts that were precious.

LUCIFER
They were august and righteous to the citizens they administered.
They cultivated Africa, the Middle East, and Asia, and ministered
Unto their subjects, to my dismay, your commandments,
Instead of brutalizing them as did the ill governments
Of Rome and Greece, when they, on the pinnacle of power,
Did in their heydays over the entire world majestically tower.

CHRIST
Rulers who fear and love me, and practice obediently my commandment
Will lead their nations with compassion, love, and fairness of judgment.
Those who follow you, nevertheless, become cruel,
And let loose misery on the helpless people they rule.

LUCIFER
Of course, they have to be
Like me, if they follow me.

(pause)

Even though my followers keep the people they rule poor and famished,
They themselves live in glamour and luxury. But yours are impoverished. .
Look at your poverty-stricken children—-Your
Children, compared with mine, are very poor.
Theoretically, since you are King of Kings owning the entire
Universe, your children should've been richer. But they retire
Poor if they ever get employed. It's ironic that those that bear your name
Are the most miserable in the world. Why is it so?.... Isn't it a shame?

CHRIST
Mine are poor because yours possess the world's wealth being greedy.
Yes, my children suffer from misery, and most of the time, are needy.
But if they pray unto me fervently for the things they need most,
And those things are good for them, I'll give them without any cost.

Yours is conditional and has a baggage
Attached to it. You compel them to engage
In your Satanic worship. All of them trade their precious
Soul for the perishable things of this world. It's vicious.
Though mine are poor in this life, they'll be
Royals in the next life in heaven with me.
Moreover, when your children die, they can't take with them their gold,
Let alone their souls that you torture and enslave because they've sold
Them to you. I advise all my children not to toil in order to save
Perishable things, but to save their souls, being wise and brave.
And if riches hinder them from going to my beautiful heaven, which
Is horrible, they'd rather be poor and go to heaven than hell, being rich.
I'd rather have them store their wealth in heaven where they don't deal
With robbers, where there's no loss, but gain; and no thieves that steal.
Being achiever in life is not being wealthy, but being rich in the knowledge
Of God, in His worship and service, and being free from spiritual bondage.

(pause)

LUCIFER
Yes, if they'd listen to your good advice.
But most humans fall for my subtle vice.
Some men even wonder why you allow us to impoverish
Millions. It's true—- We cause many to starve and perish.

CHRIST
Am I not the Creator of gold and silver, which men mine?
Is not the rich treasure of the entire Universe mine?
And didn't I generously give this to all human beings freely?
Aren't your children keeping it all to themselves greedily?
Am I to blame really for the rampant, grinding poverty
And the suffering of men and the loss of their liberty?
Am I in the business of saving souls, or am I in distribution of property?
Should I desire to distribute wealth your children have robbed in stealth,
Or in broad daylight, I've to obliterate them all and give the stolen wealth
Back to the needy. I don't want to do so now even though I'm capable
Of extricating your avaricious accomplices. I've to follow my timetable.
When my time is up, however, I'll destroy the avaricious; and the meek
Shall inherit the Earth forevermore. That's the kind of justice I'll seek.

LUCIFER
I'm afraid of your Judgment Day,
For I know it's not far away.

CHIRST
Let's discuss your present. Will your economic system be capitalism still?

LUCIFER
It'll be socialism; call it communism, if you will.
Our next step is to add to it a religion bearing my name—- Luciferism.
Those stupid boys, Marx, Lenin, Stalin and Mao imposed atheism
On their people, while they themselves were practicing Satanism.
Though I'm happy they made Russia, China and the world godless,
I'm displeased that they made everyone religion-less, nevertheless.
I like godlessness to the extent that you, God, don't become the object
Of worship. But when my existence is ignored totally, I fervidly object
Godlessness. We've been successful with our socio-economical formation.
This is the first experimental, socio-economic, and political transformation.
Soon, we'll launch our communism globally, spicing it up with my religion.
Then, we'll nationalize the world's natural resources dividing it by region.
Then, we'll have one world government, economic system, army, and religion.
Then, I, only I, will be the center of undivided attention, worship, and adoration
Till you destroy me forevermore in that Fiery Lake where there's no restoration.

CHRIST
But Russia and her allies, and even China are quitting communism,
How can you take them back to communism with your Luciferism?

LUCIFER
The Big War will bring down all to their knees and they'll accept communism
And Luciferism. Add to this my magical power that'll allure them like prism.
Also, we've to remember that even when it seemed the communist vehicle
Was running itself, we were behind its wheel steering it straight or in a circle.
We're now steering it towards a path where it seems there's no border
Between us, so that we can stealthily launch the New World Order.

(pause)

On the one hand, my children and I are indebted much to Mao and Lenin
For volunteering to conduct an experiment on their people. Joseph Stalin
Too, is unforgettable. My children from England, Germany, the Unites States,
Italy, and France weren't willing to experiment on their own people and estates.
They didn't want to endure the awful revolutions, bloodshed, and torture.
So, they shipped them to Russia and China inflicting on them their ill adventure.

CHRIST
You won't find it easy to convert the existing capitalist
Countries to communism. Expect that they'll resist.

LUCIFER
Again, that's where the Third World War comes into play.
In the aftermath of the terrific catastrophe, we will display
And lay down forcefully the program of the New World Order.
The survivors have to abide strictly by it when we give order.
Without this War, we can scream till the sky's green and the grass blue,
But still, nothing would happen, and our scream won't yield any clue
About our predicament
At this present moment.
It's as simple
As a dimple.

CHRIST
Your children feel that they got it made. They think they're smarter than all
Because they've access to your diabolical knowledge. Do they know their fall
Will be earth-shattering for going to bed with you? Do they know ever
They're rushing to the Lake of Fire when they're hurrying to take over
The world. Have you ever discussed the Lake of Fire when you meet?

LUCIFER
Am I crazy to do that? No bare, bitter things on my table; all's coated sweet.
They don't care about life after death. They're frantic to have world government.
They pursue only temporary gains and pleasure, and live the illusory moment.
They're like a cattle that see only the green grass on the surface standing tall,
Without eyeing the bottomless chasm under the grass, in which they could fall.

CHRIST
This proves that they're very shortsighted and foolish, however they think all
To be successful in this transient world. When you mercilessly trash their soul
In the next world wreaking on them untold pain, they'll realize as they calculate
Their loss, that you've deceived them craftily. Tragically, it'll then be too late.
It doesn't matter whether your children are scientists, philosophers,
Scholars, actors, statesmen, nobles, rich or poor; they're all losers.

LUCIFER
Speaking of philosophers, most of them don't admit you're the origin of things,
And that you're particularly the origin and destination of all human beings.

CHRIST
True, I'm the origin of everything and men, and I was supposed
To be, in principle, the destination of humans; but you opposed
Me, and man's free will diverted man's destination, in abomination.
So, to your followers, the Lake of Fire and you, are their destination.
As things stand now, I'm origin and destination only
Of those that believe in me, and love me genuinely.

LUCIFER
I pity all those foolish philosophers who wasted their lives trying to fathom
Whether all existence originated from water, fire, air, soil or simple atom.
For them, to think the universe originated from you was to grasp a phantom.
Some of them came close to you when they said there was a Form or Force
That created the Universe, and that everything was its reflection, of course.

CHRIST
Yes, they were unknowingly or subconsciously struggling to grasp my reality,
In any case, to return to you sarcasm, which specific philosophers do you pity

LUCIFER
All of them, be they modern or of antiquity.
I laugh at Anaximander, Thales, Socrates, Plato, Aristotle and all the Greek
Philosophers that suddenly woke up from there deep slumber and did seek
You subconsciously, after you'd already revealed yourself and your creation
To us angels, to Enoch the prophet, to Melchizedek, Ethiop and the nation
Of Israel thousands of years earlier. Obviously, the Greeks didn't read
All those ancient books by Enoch and others. The Greeks did tread
On a new and narrow philosophical path before examining and reviewing
The prevalent literature. Had they done so, the way they were viewing
God, creation, and the Universe,
Would've been the reverse.
The Greek philosophy is a recent phenomenon.
Before the rise of Alexander, there was little or none.
The fact philosophers wreak their brains to fathom whether a god was able
To create the Universe, is, for us who had seen you create it, laughable.

(pause)

Philosophers of old cannot be blamed as they didn't know your essence.
Today's philosophers know a lot about you but ignore your existence.
For them, to accept you as the origin of the universe, is too simplistic.
They've to make things too complex, too abstract, and too unrealistic
To sound like philosophers and to get accepted. Yet, every philosopher,
Even if he believes he's an independent thinker, is influenced by Lucifer.

Today's philosophers and Occidental intellectuals think that there's nothing
New about you, and seek new doctrines and religions elsewhere, forgetting
That you're new and fresh eternally, and that only you, are Truth everlasting.
Which's why Western men and women flock to India and Tibet to do fasting
And meditation that lead nowhere, but to me and to hell, as you are the Gate,
The only Gate to heaven, if they were honestly willing the Truth to investigate.

Lucifer laughs.

Running from you and the Occident, they end up with me in the Orient.
They've no clue I'm the god of their new gods, very sleek, and ancient.

Lucifer pauses with an air of self-pride before he continues speaking.

I got mad Nietzsche to dare say that you're dead, by uttering , "God is dead"
Indeed you've died for men. But he meant you didn't exist. I put in his head
The idea of the "Super Man", so that my servant, Hitler, and his "super race"
Concept, craze Germans. I, too, have plans—-I make a philosopher embrace
First any of my poisonous ideas, and find a volunteer mad man
Who'll implement my poisonous ideas and fulfill my vicious plan.
That's exactly what I did to Weishaupt, Marx, Lenin, Stalin, Mao, Trotsky,
And their followers, to make them shed blood, spread atheism and anarchy.

(pause)

I love all the existentialist philosophers including Jean Paul Sartre who blurred
You and your work, saying, "existence is meaningless, hopeless, and absurd."

(pause)

CHRIST
You spoke only half the truth when you said every philosopher
Was influenced by you, Lucifer. There are some you didn't refer.
For instance, you were unable to influence going against my divine
Will, Augustine, Aquinas, and Descartes, because they were mine.
Surely, you couldn't influence negatively even
Socrates and Plato, whose ideas are interwoven.
Your priest, Marx, snatched from my servant, Hegel, dialectics of nature
And applied it to society. Hegel acknowledged I created every creature.
You and your priest denied that I was the one that did the first
Push to the Universe, and negated that all things out of me burst.

LUCIFER
It's true... Of course, the first three wise philosophers lived in your
Christian Era. They were your faithful children—-simple and pure.

You made Descartes a genius. You taught him in his dream.
Reality and dream became one to him. That was extreme.
My philosophers blurred reality and doubted their own existence.
He said, "I think. Therefore, I exist." He proved being's essence.
He, Augustine and Aquinas defended you in the absence
Of many Christian philosophers; and proved your existence.
And I couldn't influence negatively Socrates and Plato indeed.
I admire Socrates' dying fearlessly for his truth. He did succeed
In living in his death—- In his disciple, Plato, sprouted his seed.

CHRIST
But you grabbed from Plato's *Republic* the idea that, instead of the people,
Philosophers rule. You inspired your children to adhere by this principle.

LUCIFER
This is absolutely true. That's why my elites feel that they're entitled
To take over the world and rule it. For them, this question is settled.

(after a laughter)

My elites are farther from being genuine philosophers.
If they were philosophers indeed, they'd hate to rule others.
True philosophers seek neither to rule nor be ruled in any land.
They neither lead nor follow. They'd rather walk hand in hand.

CHRIST
Oh, deceptive, sly, and old Lucifer!
Now you sound like a philosopher.

LUCIFER
Just remembered Heraclitus. He was a pure genius. He stands out among
All philosophers, frankly. His original teaching is really like a sweet song.
He nailed it right on the mark when he did state
That everything is in flux, in a constant mobile state;
And when he said correctly, I "can't step in the same river twice",
Because fresh water flows continuously. Others thought otherwise.
He was right on the mark when he revealed to all that old age
And youth, and death and life, were inseparable. What a sage!
You showed him conspicuously the dialectic of nature,
And he realized that everything had an opposing feature—
For male, female, for negative, positive, and for light, darkness.
He enlightened the dark world with such clarity and starkness.
He admitted boldly that it was you who held together and united
Opposites harmoniously... It was Heraclitus who, in truth, ignited

145

The mind of Hegel. But Hegel himself discovered nothing new.
He simply reworded in a different format everything he knew
And learned from Heraclitus himself, by describing his dialectic
As "thesis, antithesis and synthesis", and making it systematic.
Heraclitus pinpointed you by name calling you the Logos or the Word,
And introduced you as the Creator of the Universe. This was unheard
Of hitherto among the thinkers of those regions. Even your disciple,
Saint John, got the idea of the Logos or the Word from him. People
Don't realize this. He was the king of philosophers. You made Heraclitus
The unsurpassed genius that he was. The credit should go to you thus.
But those who came after him including Socrates, Aristotle, Plato, and all,
Made you vague calling you the Forms, the One ... He's the tallest of the tall.

Referring to you, John says, "in the beginning was the Word Logos,
And the Word was with God, and He was God..." That's how it goes;
Isn't it? John added, "Everything that was made was made by
Him"... Didn't Heraclitus say something like this? That's why
I say he is the greatest among philosophers, a visionary
And mystic. On top of that, he is a thinker extraordinary.

CHRIST
I'm glad you admit now that Heraclitus outshone
All present-day philosophers and those who're bygone.

LUCIFER
Lord God, can I ask you a question?

CHIRST
Ask me without hesitation.

LUCIFER
Thank you. What do you think of Martin Luther King? I mean the former;
The one that had been a Catholic before becoming a protestant reformer.

CHRIST
Let me hear what you think.

LUCIFER
(pointing at the seal and portrait of Martin Luther King)
You do know he had some link
With me. Look at his seal—-
It witnesses against him. It's big deal!
His portrait too, with his right hand on his heart
Is a sign of loyalty to me. Undeniably, he was a part

And parcel of my secret society, a Rosicrucian initiate,
Which you, my Lord, won't absolutely appreciate.
As far as I'm concerned he was my obedient servant. I claim
Him. Moreover, even if he had the right to criticize and blame
The Roman Catholic Church for the ill practices I had made it commit,
He should've reformed it from within instead of breaking away from it

In a contemptuous rebellion and revolutionary protest.
By doing what he did, I think he flunked flat his test.
In any case, I've benefited much from his radical rebellion
And secession—- behold, your church is divided into a billion
Segments. I feel the pain you endure because of the division of your church.
But you're one God, indivisible, and your salvation is one. A simple research
On the state of your present church proves that it is unbelievably tragic.
Martin Luther King is responsible for this division inexplicable by logic.
I attempted to capture his soul on his death-bed, but Raphael pushed
Me aside and took him with him; I hope, not to Paradise. I wished
To take him with me. I was going to protest, but Raphael muzzled
My mouth. Where's my Martin Luther King? I'm really puzzled...

CHRIST
You really love to accuse
Without mercy or excuse!
(with a smile of sarcasm)
So, you're concerned for my church?...Yes, I've heard what you have to say.
Regarding Martin Luther King, I'll reserve his whole case till Judgment Day.
He didn't intend to split the church in the beginning. He begged audience
With the Pope, but was denied. One way or another he expressed obedience
To the Pope and the Catholic Church. He wrote what he thought was wrong,
But could not renounce his conscience's dictates. He was denounced among
His fellow Catholics. Yes, it's true; he indulged with you in occult for a while.
Yet, he repented before he died. We've kept his wrongs and rights in his file.

Even though we're very sad about our church's conflict and division,
The way things were going, it was inevitable, according to our vision,
That sooner or later, one way or another,
The church would've ceased to be together.
It's true, Martin Luther King was not a perfect man.
But he did good in translating my Bible into German.
Thus making it available to the German common man.
He has done both good and bad. He begged our pardon. He did repent.
We forgave him. We're merciful to the repenting, unlike you, the serpent.
There are many others like Martin Luther King with divine
Forgiveness, who appear to be yours, but are actually mine.

On the Judgment Day, his file will be opened like everyone's file.
Hence, accuser, I advise you to stop your accusation, meanwhile.

LUCIFER
(embarrassed a bit)
There are also pastors and evangelists with many a miracle and sign,
That seem to be yours in the eyes of the public, but are actually mine.
If I were to compile a long list of their names and reveal
Them, the world will be shocked; and the hurt can't heal.

CHRIST
Why don't you go ahead and reveal their identity?

LUCIFER
(with a smile)
Who'll be left to serve me if I expose each and every entity?
My secrecy is the secret of my power and success, in reality.

(pause)

If it's not repeating myself or the same thing,
It still hurts me that I lost Martin Luther King .
I'll wait till Judgment Day,
If you, Lord God, so say.

(pause)

How about philosopher Bertrand Russell,
Who showed you his tongue's muscle?

CHRIST
What about Bertrand Russell?

LUCIFER
Bertrand Russell not only hated you, but disrespected
You. His attitude towards you was not really expected
From one who claimed to be a philosopher. He criticized you in a spree
Of insults for cursing the fig that didn't bear fruit. Your cursing the tree
For not bearing fruit, according to him, did not stand to reason,
Because you demanded fruits from the tree in the wrong season.
Oh, my!... He even dared call you "stupid" and another shocking name.
He was an arrogant and ignorant man full of hate and unthinkable shame.
How did he, a feeble, mortal man, have the audacity to insult
God Almighty? I'm presently torturing him in hell, as a result.

(pause)

What that fool didn't know was that, using the tree as an example, along the way,
You wanted to teach that a person who didn't bear fruit in you, will wither away.
For saying that you, who made time and created trees, didn't know the season,
And for insulting you with his filthy mouth, I'm torturing him in my prison.

CHRIST
(with a chuckle)
Hmm… because you care for me so much, which's beyond reason,
You're torturing Bertrand Russell in the dungeon of your prison?…

LUCIFER
Exactly!… Russell knew enough about you, but denied your existence
So that he could indulge in promiscuity and drunkenness, for instance.
He thought that he would be at absolute liberty
To do whatever he liked by denying your true reality,
Unaware that you and I were watching his immorality.

CHRIST
(calmly)
You hate him because he denied your existence, and didn't humiliate
Himself by prostrating to you. You imprisoned him in hell to retaliate.
But then again, even if Russell worshiped you and did adore
You, you wouldn't ease his pain. You'd torture him even more,
As we, sadly, couldn't keep and protect him in Paradise,
Because he ridiculed and rejected us thinking he was wise.

LUCIFER
(feeling uneasy)
I admit… Yes, what you said is true.
It was not because I cared for you…

CHRIST
O, tempter and accuser, I heard you.
You said what's false and also true.
You've expressed all your whims, ill-wishes, and futility.
It's up to me whether I'll allow you to exercise them in reality…

Being transported into the 21st Century,
You saw clearly your influence on history.
That's how it goes when you move forward in time and decipher
The past and the 21st Century. Now, however, get out of it, Lucifer.

Lucifer comes back to the time where he had left off.

CHRIST
(to Lucifer and the other fallen angels)
Whatever I needed to tell you, you've heard. Nothing have you missed.
Until the day I feel like talking to you again, all of you are dismissed.

The disgraced angels go their way.

Christ remains quiet and watches like a vision His birth on Earth, His painful crucifixion, death, resurrection, and ascension to heaven. He becomes pensive for a while. His angels wonder what is going on with Him.

Let's go. I just had a glimpse of my birth,
Life, death, and resurrection on this Earth.
Verily, verily, it's inevitable...
But again, I've a timetable....

FADE OUT.

FADE IN:

One thousand years after God has created the first human beings, their descendants become many in number and live in different cities that have flourished. God visits the cities and people and is pleased with what He sees. He congratulates the first human beings who are one thousand years old and heralds to them that it is about time to return home, to the Fifth Heaven, and join Him there while they are still alive, since they didn't sin to deserve death. He transfigures them and endows them with glorified bodies.

CHRIST
Like I prepared you one year ago,
Today is the day in which you'll go
Back home, I am pleased with your achievements.
You've lived in accordance with my commandments.
All these years you walked with me uprightly every inch.
The enemy attempted to stray you, but you didn't flinch.
You've successfully accomplished your earthly task.
Today is your day of honor—you will certainly bask
In the light of my majestic glory you had known before.
Bid your children and grandchildren farewell, therefore.
(looking at the children)
If your children too walk with me hand in hand,
I'll bless them, their animals, and also their land.
And when they accomplish their noble, earthly mission,
They too will be taken alive to heaven with my permission.
Over millions of years, you'll be parents of quite many races,
Which, due to climate, will be white, dark, and yellow faces.
The further they move away from the sun, they'll get lighter
By complexion. This'll affect their melanin, which shall alter.

ONE OF THE CROWD
We promise we will walk with you all the way.
Yes, we'll stick with you, we won't stray away!

LUCIFER
(invisible to the people)
Oh, yeah! You've to prove that yet.
I'll get you soon . . . You want to bet?

CHRIST
(ignoring Lucifer and observing the area)
You've made such wonderful houses and tools.
You're so inventive and do things by the rules.
It excites and intrigues me to see people I've created
Themselves creating things that could be highly rated.

151

It thrills me to see the range of your creativities
When your talents expand as you grow as entities.
Would that you won't abuse your talents and inventions!
Would that you use your inventions for good intentions!

LUCIFER
(to himself)
They'll never think good as long as I'm around.
I'll make them evil and guaranteed—hell bound.

THE SECOND OF THE CROWD
We will not abuse our talents and inventions,
Lord! We will use them for good intentions!

CHRIST
(to the first fourteen human beings)
Let's go! I'll now give you glorified bodies suitable
For heaven. You'll have dinner today at my table.

Christ stretches His right hand towards them, and they translate into celestial beings and ascend to Aryam, the Fifth Heaven, with Christ and the angels, while their children and grandchildren watch them with tearful eyes.

LUCIFER
I can't believe they made it! I'll on myself spit,
If I don't drag their children down the fiery pit.

FADE OUT.

FADE IN:

Indeed, millions of years pass by and Satan succeeds to mislead the descendants of the first human beings. As a result, when Christ is about to destroy people in the First Earth Age, mankind, having reached the climax of its civilization over millions of years having built cities, skyscrapers, machines, electricity, air and space crafts, is on the verge of extinction due to decadence, class oppression, injustice of all sorts, racism, ethnic conflicts, Satanism, witchcraft, and sexual perversion, because of the influence of Lucifer and the other fallen angels. Christ finds only seven righteous families in every corner of the world. He plans to send his angels to protect and to lead these people to shelters and to destroy the rest by earthquakes and volcanoes.

ANGLE ON CHRIST.

CHRIST
My angels, as you see, Earth has been corrupted by Lucifer.
All are defiled by him—men, and animals with or without fur.
There are only seven families that have been prominent,
Because they haven't worshiped Satan. So, it's eminent
That we should save them, lest their races become extinct.
Let's shelter them under Earth, as they're indeed distinct.
After we annihilate the evil people who cause us pain,
With their survivors, we will start life all over again.
As you have witnessed, though we kindly gave man knowledge
To build cities and flying machines, he's pushed us to the edge
Shedding innocent blood, committing injustice, perversion,
Practicing viciously Satanism and witchcraft without aversion.
Our patience is brimful. We've reversed our earliest intentions.
We'll now mercilessly destroy him and also his evil inventions.

GABRIEL
Our God knows what He does. His judgment's just and fair.
Who's like He? He even knows the number of man's hair.

CHRIST
(to His Archangels)
Save those seven families and animals of their kind,
And annihilate the rest of the animals and mankind!

Fourteen angels lead in a hurry the seven families and animals of their kind to underground shelters. Four angels who have power to cause volcanoes and earthquakes stand at the four corners of the world, drawing high up their flaming swords. When they move their swords, a massive worldwide volcano erupts, burning men, animals, and cities to ashes. When the molten lava cools off and the earth is once again habitable, the angels bring the people out of the shelters. They remind them that the world was destroyed because of sin and warn them not to sin by worshiping Lucifer, practicing witchcraft, killing each other in the name of war, and committing sexual perversion, lest they kindle the wrath of God again. The survivors, who become the progenitors of the" black, white, and yellow races", walk with God in their lifetimes. However, their descendants start to sin again, disappointing God. Thousands of years pass by, and the people completely forget God. So, He makes plans to go down to Earth and settle the problem of sin once and for all. To this end, He prepares to form a different breed of a human being from the dust, a human being who has nothing to do with the rest of the old human races that were corrupted by Satanic influences at that time, in spite of the fact their ancestors had been created by the Word of God from earth, fire, wind, and water, in the same way the Word (Christ) had created the stars, the suns, and moons only by speaking and saying, "let there be light" etc. They are unlike the new and recent man called Adam whom he fashioned with his own fingers out of pure dust and granted him life by breathing in his nostrils. Looking in retrospect from the twenty-first century, it took place as recently as about eight thousand years ago, compared to the first human beings who were created in greater numbers much earlier than that (over three million years ago, according to the oldest human bones found in Ethiopia called Luci by Westerns and Dinknesh by Ethiopians). They were created completely whole, in pairs as males and females (Genesis, Chapter 1:27), as opposed to one man (Adam) who was formed (molded) out of dust as a single and lonely individual who became a living soul only after God breathed life in his nostrils. (Genesis 2:7). This is my understanding of these verses. If you disagree with me, dear reader, ignore my contention and entertain your own views of them, and we will still be friends. The bottom line is that it was one and the same God that created or made everyone and everything that exists even though the times of creation may vary. We are in agreement as far as this is concerned, and that is what matters. Moreover, it is the same God, Jesus Christ, who died for mankind, who rose from the dead, and who will return to judge the world, irrespective of my or your interpretation of Genesis or any part of the Bible. Like I said, I have taken artistic liberty or used poetic license to comprehend the scriptures in accordance with my understanding of them. Besides, that is the only way I can explain and reconcile with the existence of physically different and unique human races in different parts of the world, as well as the finding of animal and human bones dating back millions of years. I may be wrong. But then, who knows except God, I may be right. This is pertaining to whether Adam was the first or last created(actually, formed from the dust) human being.

CHRIST
(to His archangels)

Eventually, I, myself, have to descend to Earth to save humanity.
I've to be a human being to stop these evil profanity and insanity.
But I can't be born from the union of just any man and woman—
One way or another all have been defiled by Satan. Rather than
Use the old man, I will form a new man from dust,
From whose seeds I'll be born someday. It's a must
That I empty myself of my glory and be born only from his seed.
I'll separate and sanctify his seed lest they mix with Satan's weed.
He will be misled indirectly by Satan, but the new man
Won't worship him. Using his seed, I can fulfill my plan.
Moreover, he'll repent his sin and beg for my mercy.
Yet, it's only by my own death he'll receive clemency,
Till my enemy misleads him, this man will be innocent like a lamb.
He'll have a wife called Eve who'll push him to sin. I call him Adam.

I'll keep him in seclusion in Paradise, the heavenly garden,
To protect him from others, making him Paradise's warden.
(repeating himself for emphasis)
Yes, this Garden, as you know, is situated in Paradise, located in Iyor,
The Third Heaven, whose replica on Earth will be called by men for
A long time as the "Garden of Eden." For sure, it is its reflection.
Compared with the heavenly Paradise, the earthly lacks perfection.
By the same token, my heavenly Jerusalem is fantastic and perfect.
But its reflection, Melchizedek's earthly Jerusalem, will have defect.
(to Michael and Raguel)
Look at Adam's model. I want his joy to brim . . .
He's awesome, isn't he? Tell me how you find him.

RAGUEL
He's fabulous!

MICHAEL
When Lucifer sees him, he'd be jealous!

GABRIEL
He's so gorgeous!

CHRIST
I'll duplicate his mold on Earth and form it into a living soul
When I breathe life in his nostrils to make him a perfect whole.

MICHAEL
I haven't quite understood about this new man and his seed.

RAGUEL
Me too, Lord. This new man is exciting and intriguing indeed.

CHRIST
(to Michael)
As you know, Lucifer has corrupted again the entire earth.
All humans have turned against us in every house and hearth.
Though we've destroyed city upon city,
Men don't repent feeling guilty and pity.
In our sight, they're all abominable and unholy,
Causing a tragic state of sorrow and melancholy.
It's hard to use anyone of their bodies to descend
To become flesh, dwell amongst them in the end
To be punished in their place and save them by grace;
For, they've all become a rebellious and Satanic race.

We will, therefore, make a totally new breed
Of people, sanctified for us, from whose seed
Like I said, I have to be born and save humanity
From perishing without a trace in hell for eternity.
I'll lull Adam into a deep sleep, operate his side,
Extract a bone out of his rib, turn it into a bride,
And give her to him to be his companion and wife.
Because, without a companion, he'll be lonely in life.
Both being flesh of the same flesh, they will unite,
Becoming one whole, and their love being infinite.

MICHAEL
Lord, will Adam be black or white?

CHRIST
He will be like dawn, neither completely dark nor light.
I'll show them mercy and bear with them, since I'll elect
Their remnants to be my priests through whom I can collect
My other children scattered all over the planet,
To set them free from Lucifer's fetter and net.

GABRIEL
May death be far from you, Lord!

PHANUEL
May your enemy die from the same sword!

RAGUEL
What exactly would the nature of Adam's sin be?

CHRIST
Lucifer will entice him to eat of a forbidden tree.

RAGUEL
Lord, since you know before it happens
That Adam will fall surely when he opens
His heart to Lucifer's lies, why would you command
Him not to eat of a forbidden tree, on the other hand?

CHRIST
The very fact that I can foretell the outcome in precision
Of man's future decision, has no bearing on his decision.
As far as man is concerned, there is a probability
That he might decide rightly, though the possibility

That he might decide otherwise is indeed higher
Than the impossibility, because of his heart's desire.
In other words, my foreknowledge of events doesn't control
Man's actions. Man sets his life's course, playing in it a role.
And yet, I've to make man aware of my impending judgments
Of the consequences of breaking my laws and commandments.
For instance, I'll set light and darkness, life and death before
Him, to choose light over darkness, life over death. Therefore,
Using his free will, it's up to him to choose wisely that or this.
I'll advise him to choose the good, but the final decision is his.

MICHAEL
Lord, is your terrific death really man's worth?
Isn't there any other solution you can bring forth?

CHRIST
It was decided long before the foundation of the Earth,
I love man exceedingly—my terrific death is his worth.
Let's go to Elda, which's in the future Ethiopia. It's a nice
Garden. I will form Adam there and place him in Paradise.

FADE OUT.

FADE IN:

Christ and His angels go down to Elda, a place located near the earthly Garden of Eden, in what is now called Ethiopia. This place exists in Ethiopia at the present time with a different name. Now it is called Damot (eda-mot), meaning "death is a burden," referring to the death of Adam and Eve. In those days, it was a secluded area with multicolored flowers, rivulets, and vines. Even though the present Ethiopia was not then called Ethiopia, God calls it so, for God is timeless and sees the past and future as now and here.

RAPHAEL

Lord, who can question your wisdom? You're the wisest of the wise.
Forgive me for asking this—why don't you form Adam in Paradise?

CHRIST

Paradise is holy. As you know, it's not common and simple.
One has to be perfect and holy to enter it as in a holy temple.
It has to do with the law of cleansing lasting forty
Days for men, and eighty for women, to attain purity.
I'll command their seeds too, to observe this cardinal principle
Regarding sexual purity, child birth, and my future holy temple.
So, we'll keep him forty days, and her eighty, in this place of purity
Before we allow them to enter holy and sacred Paradise with surety.
Furthermore, as both of them will be banished from Paradise
To Elda, the place of their birth, it'd lessen their shock and surprise.
Since we'll form them on Earth from dust, it'd be appropriate and just
To return them to Earth, where, when they die, they become again dust.

While the good angels look from close proximity, and Lucifer and the fallen angels watch from afar, Christ molds Adam tenderly and lovingly from earth, fire, wind, and water. Then He breathes in his nostrils, and he becomes a living, thirty-years old man, who is able to reason and speak perfectly, right away. His mind reflects brilliance. He exhibits exuberance.

CHRIST
Wake up, Adam!

ADAM
(opening his eyes slowly)
Lord God, I am . . .

Adam stands and praises God in a song:

I adore you, my God: who, but you can raise
A living being out of lifeless dust? O! I praise
You eternally and worship you for transforming
A dust like myself into an honorable being, forming

158

Me so tenderly and so lovingly with your fingers divine,
Placing me among these fabulous rivulets, trees, and vine!
Hitherto, I was indeed nothing but lifeless earth,
Good only for treading upon, without any worth,
Until you made me man forming me in your image.
How can I pay back? My praise is my only homage—
Praise after praise, praise of adoration!
Praise of appreciation and admiration!

CHRIST
You think these flowers, trees, vines, and rivulets are nice?
You haven't seen anything yet; wait till you get to Paradise!

LUCIFER
(to his lieutenants)
My! My! This creature is so gorgeous! God took His precious
Time to form him! Oh, how lucky is this man! Oh, I'm jealous!

AZAZEL
If we can get him somehow, friends, we can hurt God so hard!

ANNANEL
Hurt the man too. We will get him as God won't be his guard!

Christ instructs His angels to construct a temporary shelter for Adam, until he is permitted to enter Paradise, located in the Third Heaven.

CHRIST
(to his angels)
Build him a temporary shelter quickly.
And make him a fence wooded thickly.

The angels do as commanded by their God, and Adam moves into the shelter.

FADE OUT.

FADE IN:

EXT. ELDA. DAY.
Forty days after his creation, Adam is walking in his fenced garden. Christ and his angels come to take him to the heavenly Paradise. Because Adam now has a glorified body undefiled by sin, he is capable of "flying,", that is, moving through space and matter unhindered.

CHRIST
Come, my beloved Adam, let's go to the heavenly Paradise. Hold
My hand. We'll travel through space. You'll learn to fly. Be bold.

Adam holds the hand of Christ with uncertainty and fear. They move out of Elda to the heavenly Paradise followed by the angels. Adam looks around Paradise with a great surprise and excitement.

ADAM
What a wonderful place! Thank you so much, Lord!
In such a Paradise, I don't think I'll ever get bored.

CHRIST
You're welcome! *(to the angels)* Build him a permanent house
With strong fence. Make enough rooms for him and his spouse.

The angels do as told by Christ.

CHRIST
(to Adam, pointing at the wood)
Live here and eat of the fruits of every tree in this wood,
My dear, except the Tree of Knowledge of evil and good
Which is in the center. Beware, son! You shall neither touch it
Nor even go close to it. You'll surely die if you taste even a bit
Of it. You'll die spiritually and physically being cut off from God.
And your sin will pass on to your descendants as a spiritual load.
But if you observe my commandment remembering your Creator,
I will take you alive to my Heavenly Jerusalem, many years later.
If anyone persuades you to eat it, resist without hesitation,
With all your might, and you shall overcome the temptation.
You'll lose fellowship with me if you sin.
If you resist sin, you will definitely win
My love and affection; and I'll truly shower
Upon you my blessing every minute and hour.
Don't listen to my enemy. Resist the Devil!
He's cunning. His name is Satan. He is evil!
He's an angel cast out of heaven long ago, with disgrace.
He's misled many angels, sadly, and hates the human race.
Son, be watchful! Don't be off guard even for an instant!

ADAM
(nervously)
Lord, I will be vigilant!
I will observe your commandment.
I won't break it even for a moment.

CHRIST
Then you'll live forever. Next week we'll go to Earth. You'll name
All the animals that you will rule over, love, domesticate, and tame.
(after a pause)
Phanuel will be your guardian. He's an angel of fame.
He'll be with you right away when you call his name.

PHANUEL
Absolutely. Call me any time. Defying distance and space,
Oh, dearest Adam, I will swiftly fly and be at your place.

ADAM
Thank you much, Phanuel, servant of the Most High God.
I will definitely call you if I feel something weird or odd.

MOVING SHOT.
As Christ and his angels walk away from Adam, they meet Lucifer and his angels who look dirty and miserable. Lucifer, Azazel, Semazya, and Annanel tremble and prostrate to Christ. Christ is grief- stricken upon seeing their tragic looks.

LUCIFER
Aw! Have we come face to face! Greetings to our God and Lord,
Who can create and destroy with His word sharper than a sword!

CHRIST
(moved to tears by their condition)
The four of you get more miserable from epoch to epoch, age to age.
Your voice of agony grieves my spirit in spite of the untold damage
You've inflicted on us. What a stench am I smelling? It makes no sense!
Aren't you the very angels who once smelt like myrrh and frankincense,
Whose fragrance was perfume to our nose, whose sight
Was often to our divine eyes the most wonderful delight?

LUCIFER
Yes, Lord, it's us that stink like filth and that resemble dirt.
It baffles us, oh, God, that you pity us even after we've hurt
You so much! Your compassion is so unfathomable by us.
It's beyond our comprehension that you still love us thus!

CHRIST
I can control everything in this Universe, but I can't shove
And control, however hard I try, only one thing—my love
For my creatures even when they hate me much and hurt me;
For I cannot change my nature which loves even my enemy.
It's this very love that will drive me to empty myself of my
Heavenly glory, to come down to Earth, to suffer and to die.
Yea, I'm Almighty God. I have no any weakness but fervent love.
My love is beyond understanding. Yes, it's only love I can't shove.

LUCIFER
To die? How could God die?
What for? And indeed, why?

CHRIST
Why else could it be,
Except to set man free . . .

LUCIFER
(wondering how exactly God would die)
Allow me Lord God, to tempt Adam. Let me find a proof
Against him and make him guilty deserving your reproof . . .

CHRIST
It's written in the stars and heavenly tablets that you shall tempt
Him. So, be it! Go ahead and do your mischief. Make an attempt!
Yes, you can tempt him keeping yourself at a certain distance
From him. You shall touch his person under no circumstance!

Lucifer changes himself into a raven while Christ and His angels are watching, being invisible to Adam. Lucifer flies towards Adam, perches on a tree, and tempts Adam.

LUCIFER AS RAVEN
Peace, Adam! I'm a messenger from El-Shadai, the Seventh Heaven!

ADAM
(puzzled and suspicious)
Peace unto you too. Are you really from the Seventh Heaven, raven?

LUCIFER
Yes I am . . . Did God tell you that though you're its warden,
You should not eat of the tree in the middle of this garden?

ADAM
Yes. He did. He said vehemently I'll die if I eat of it.
I should neither approach it, nor even taste one bit.

LUCIFER AS RAVEN
No, no, Adam. You won't die or have any sort of demise.
If you eat of it, God knows you'll be like Him—very wise!

ADAM
(with anger and firm voice)
Are you making God a liar, raven!
Be gone! You're not from heaven!

Lucifer retreats in shame. Christ and the good angels smile and take off.

FADE OUT.

FADE IN:

EXT. PARADISE. A WEEK AFTER ADAM HAS ENTERED PARADISE. MORNING.

Christ and his angels are in Paradise, the Third Heaven, to take Adam to the earthly Garden of Eden to name the animals. At present, in the 21st Century, there is a place in Harer, Eastern Ethiopia, called "Debre Kirub", meaning "Mount of Cherub". It is called so, as legend has it, because Adam, who had the qualities of a cherub despite his humanity, named his animals on Debre Kirub (Mount Cherub.) There used to be a temple on it even as late as a few hundred years ago, built by Ethiopian believers who sought to memorialize that spot. King Mekadishi, one of the twelve Ethiopian kings that went to Bethlehem from the Ethiopian Empire to pay homage to baby Jesus, was the ruler of this region including today's Ogaden and Somalia. He prayed on Debre Kirub shortly before he left Ethiopia following a star that led him and the other kings to Bethlehem when they transported gifts to baby Jesus. Debre Kirub probably lies in ruins in Ethiopia presently.

CHRIST
Let's go to Earth. I've gathered the animals in the earthly Garden
Of Eden. You'll name them all. They're waiting for you in Eden.

MOVING SHOT.

Christ, Adam, and the angels move to the above-mentioned mountain now called "Mount Kirub" (Mount Cherub) in Ethiopia, in the then Garden of Eden, which was watered by the rivers Pishon (now called Wabi Shebele River by Ethiopians) and Gihon(the Blue Nile), both of which flow in Ethiopia to this day, as well as Hiddekel and Euphrates, which flow in today's Iraq. Christ has already gathered samples of all the animals of the earth on this mountain. Adam, who has a very intelligent mind, names the animals.

CHRIST
Name these animals, Adam.

ADAM
(touching the animals)
I'll call this one goat, this one lamb.
This one a dove, this a crow, this a bat.
This a tiger, this a lion, this one a cat . . .

While Adam names the animals, Christ bids him farewell and leaves with his angels.

CHRIST
(interrupting Adam)
Goodbye, my love. I'll come again to form your wife and partner,
to take some of the animals to Paradise, and make you its gardener.
The animals will keep you company under the sun and moon.

ADAM

I'll miss you, my God, please come back soon!

Christ and His angels leave Adam on Mount Kirub. Adam observes the animals and sees that they are male and female. He feels sad because he has no partner.

ADAM
(to himself)
All these animals are male and female. Everyone has a partner;
But I have no any partner. I am nothing but a lonely gardener.

FADE OUT.

FADE IN:

EXT. PARADISE. MORNING. A WEEK LATER.

Adam is still on Mount Kirub, playing with some of his animals. Christ approaches him with His angels.

CHRIST
How are you beloved? Are you happy with your life?

ADAM
Yes, I am, Lord! It'd be even better with a wife.
I envy my animals and despair
When I see them playing in pair.
If I had a wife, I won't despair.
All the animals of Paradise and Earth are in pair.
It's only a wife that can my broken heart repair.

CHRIST
Son, even though your voice was faint,
Being in Aryam I heard your complaint.
I know that it's not good for you to be alone.
So, I came to get you a wife out of your bone.
Because she's the bone of your bone, she'll cleave
To you. She will be your soul mate. Name her Eve.
We'll go back to Elda. I'll lull you to sleep and extract
Her from you. She'll be your match, precise and exact.

ADAM
Thank you, Lord, for your generous act!

MOVING SHOT.

They go to Elda and stand at the front yard of Adam's old house.

CHRIST
Lay down for me, Adam. Sleep and be numb for a moment.
I'll get you beautiful Eve. Your joy will fill the firmament!

While the angels of God and of Lucifer are watching in bewilderment, Adam lays down in a deep slumber. Christ takes a bone from his right rib and forms it into Eve. She is fifteen years old physically, but as brilliant as Adam mentally. Eve praises God for bringing her into existence.

EVE
I praise and worship, Almighty God, my origin and destination.
I was nothing but a sleeping bone even as a bird in hibernation,
Latent inside my man, as if I didn't exist at all. But now
I am well and alive in my own right. I don't know how!
It's just miraculous! It's beyond my comprehension!
All I can say is that it's my God's well intention!
(looking at Adam who is sound asleep)
Oh, my! Out of what a beautiful thing
Have you carved me a perfect being!
What an exquisite being ! What a perfect workmanship!
What pleasingly charming! And with him I've kinship!

LUCIFER
Wawwawwaw! She's adorable! I wish I am
That lucky being, that stupid called Adam!

AZAZEL
A miracle took place!

ANNANEL
Her face radiates light, look at her face!

Christ wakes up Adam. Adam opens his eyes and is surprised to see a beautiful woman near him.

ADAM
Who's this fantastic being that's striking my heart like lightning!
Something's moving in my heart! Don't know what's happening!

CHRIST
Rejoice, Adam! This is a good sign and start—
Love's being born and moving in your heart.

ADAM
Lord, some forceful feelings are drawing me to this being.
Is she really mine, this awesome creature that I'm seeing?

CHRIST
(with a smile)
Yes, she's yours, Adam . . . yours alone forevermore.
You two are inseparable like the sea and the shore.

ADAM
I am so glad that between us there won't be any rift!
Thank you, God, for your wonderful and precious gift!

CHRIST
You shall love each other here on Earth and in Heaven.
None is greater than the other; you're equal and even.
Multiply and fill the earth, be a mighty race.
I empower you to rule the world in my place.
Have dominion over all animals as well as nature.
Yeah! May you reign mightily over every creature!
You, beloved Eve, you will enter the heavenly Garden of Eden
Called Paradise eighty days later. Till then, stay in this garden
With Archangel Gabriel. Good will to Earth! Peace to men!

ADAM AND EVE
(kneeling and kissing Christ's feet)
Amen, Lord God! Amen!

FADE OUT.

FADE IN:

EXT. HEAVENLY PARADISE.

Eighty days after Eve's formation, Christ permits her entrance into Paradise, the Third Heaven. Christ repeats to Eve what He had previously commanded Adam to do.

CHRIST
Live in here and eat of the fruits of any tree in this wood,
Except the tempting Tree of Knowledge of evil and good,
Which's in the middle of the garden. You shall neither touch it,
Nor go close to it. You'll surely die even if you taste of it a bit.
You'll die spiritually, and even physically, being cut off
From me. If you keep my commandment and don't scoff
It, I'll fellowship with you and bless you both generously with long
Age and take you alive to Aryam, the Fifth Heaven, later. Be strong!
If anyone persuades you to eat of it, resist without hesitation,
With all your might, and you shall overcome the temptation.
You'll lose fellowship with me if you sin.
If you resist sin, you will definitely win
My love and affection, and I'll surely shower
Upon you my blessings every minute and hour.
Don't listen to my enemy. Resist the Devil!
He's cunning. His name's Satan. He is evil!
He's a vicious angel who has tumbled down from grace.
He has misled many angels and the entire human race.
Children, be watchful. Don't be off guard even for an instant!

ADAM AND EVE
Lord God, we will be vigilant.
We'll observe your commandment.
We'll not break it even for a moment!

CHRIST
Enjoy yourselves my little ones; have no fear.
Call me and I'll be here. I am far, yet near.
Goodbye, children! Resist bravely the enemy,
Yes, beloved, call me any time if you need me.

FADE OUT.

FADE IN:

EXT. A FIELD OF FLOWERS. MORNING IN PARADISE.

Adam and Eve are in a field of beautiful flowers. They are not wearing cloths as they are adorned and covered by light and glory of grace, which do not reveal their private parts. Adam gives flowers to Eve.

EVE
Hey, Adam!

ADAM
Yes, madam!

EVE
These are lovely flowers . . . Thank you love!

ADAM
You're welcome. I love you, Eve, my special gift from above!

EVE
O, beloved, when I was on Earth, I missed you a whole bunch,
As a stem is missed passionately even by its detached branch.
(after kissing him affectionately)
This place is so fantastic!

ADAM
Indeed gorgeous and majestic.

EVE
Adam, we're so lucky to be here. I love every bit of Paradise!

ADAM
You haven't seen anything yet. There's much more surprise.

They go to the Tree of Life and eat some of its fruits.

ADAM
I really enjoy eating of this Tree of life.
We have to thank God for it, dear wife.
Hmmm! It's yummy! It's the most delicious fruit in this Garden.
Eating it has no hurtful consequence. I'm proud to be its warden.

EVE
(also chewing the fruits)
How do you know that this is the most delicious fruit in this Garden?
Have you tried all the fruits in here since you've become its warden?

ADAM
You made a good point. Yes, I haven't tried all.
Nor will I ever try. I can't jump over the wall . . .

EVE
If you cannot jump over the wall, you can bring down the wall.
You've a choice. Using your free will, you can let the wall fall.

ADAM
Eve, you're so fearfully audacious! How would you dare
Suggest to bring down the wall God has erected! Beware!

EVE
Oh no, I don't mean you ought
To do it. It's a fanciful thought.

ADAM
Eve, this is serious! Don't you ever fancy that we will ever
Eat of the Tree of Knowledge. It'll never happen! Never!

Eve looks at Adam as if to say "really?" They walk away from the Tree of Life. After a long silence between them, Eve breaks the silence.

EVE
When I was on Earth, it was so real, so visible, and tangible
As Paradise, unlike God's abode, which tends to be invisible.

ADAM
Here's how it is: the invisible is as real as the visible.
In reality, it's on the invisible roots deep in the sands
That the visible stem of the palm tree firmly stands.
It's only on the invisible foundation our house's visible walls
Stand. Without the foundations, each wall crumbles and falls.
It's the unseen breath, which God breathed in us, that holds together
The frames of our bodies. Otherwise, they'll surely collapse whether
They are very weak or very strong.
To think on the contrary is wrong.
Clearly, it's the invisible God, which sustains each atom
Of the visible world, even though it's hard this to fathom.
The invisible is eternal. The visible is temporal . . .

(after a pause)
The visible is evanescent, indeed, ephemeral.
The wind's invisible and intangible; and yet, it has power to uproot
A visible, giant tree, which seems powerful, making it utterly kaput.
On Earth, God too, is invisible and also intangible.
Yet, He's capable of making or breaking the visible.
Moreover, every world is real and tangible for those who are in it.
It's only for those outside it that it seems intangible, like a spirit.

EVE
How do you know all this, Adam? I think you know much.

ADAM
We both know the same. God makes me say such and such.

EVE
I think knowledge is good. I wish I know a whole bunch!
(thinking of the Tree of Knowledge)
The Tree of Knowledge intrigues me much. I'm already curious!

ADAM
I too! Since God made a big deal of it, it must be something serious.

EVE
We shouldn't be afraid at least to look at it from close proximity.

ADAM
(with a fearful voice)
It's dangerous! What if it gravitates and strikes us with affinity?

EVE
Well, to avert sinking in a sea of trouble for infinity,
We shouldn't get close enough and develop affinity.

They go and fix their gaze on the Tree of Knowledge.

Lucifer and his angels appear behind them invisibly, get too close to them, and charge their minds.

LUCIFER
(to both of them in a whisper)
Don't chicken, eat of the Tree of Knowledge,
And free yourselves from God's bondage!

EVE
(profoundly enchanted by the tree)
Oh, my! my! . . . simply awesome!
I really wish I could have some!
My mouth is watering! I can't believe it! Listen to my heartbeat!

ADAM
Something in me urges me to eat it! It says, "Don't chicken, eat!"

EVE
(her mouth dripping)
I feel the same way! Oh, it's magical! It's eatable!
Oh, it's irresistible like a savory food on a table!

She walks straight to the tree and stands very close to it without realizing her action.

ADAM
We better turn back and run!
Oh, my gash, this is not fun!

They run away swiftly to a different direction.

EVE
Why did God make this tree so special?
Unlike the rest, it's tempting and crucial!

ADAM
I believe Almighty God put us both in such a difficulty in order
To test our obedience and loyalty by drawing a tempting border.

EVE
It's such a hard test!

ADAM
Which disturbs peace and rest!

EVE
I wish we could eat of it to see what'd happen,
My dear husband, when our blind eyes open.

ADAM
I prefer the Tree of Life. We'd rather eat of the Tree of Life,
As we've always done, and live forevermore, dearest wife.

EVE
What's the point of living in darkness for the sake of eternal endurance?
I'd rather live in the light even for a day, than live forever in ignorance.
Besides, the Tree of Life isn't interesting, for we've been easily able
To eat of it when we so desired, as it's freely accessible and available.

ADAM
We're in dilemma—we've to choose between death and life, dear wife.
We've a free will to choose one. How can we choose death over life?

FADE OUT.

FADE IN:

EXT. UNDER THE SHADE OF THE TREE OF KNOWLEDGE. BEFORE NOON.

Lucifer and his angels are sitting under the shade of the Tree of Knowledge.

ANGLE ON LUCIFER.

LUCIFER
(looking at the Tree briefly)
O, you forbidden fruit leading to forbidden knowledge!
Man's craving for the unknown pushes him to the edge.
If sheer curiosity and the forbidden knowledge to death lead indeed,
There's a realm of knowledge beyond which man shouldn't proceed;
Realm of knowledge reserved for God only, whose quintessence
Only He fathoms. Should man mess with it, suffers the consequence.
When curiosity seizes man, he flirts with death, let alone fear death;
And craves for death to see what really happens after his last breath.
Yet, God's monopoly of knowledge isn't so fair,
For it leaves ignorant man with fear and despair.
I've enticed and allured man now for so many years,
Causing destruction, havoc, rivers of blood, and tears.
I, Lucifer, who was once the glory of heaven, the bright morning star,
That inflicted the worlds with incurable pain and a deep, deep scar.
I, who mesmerized God's own angels and stole
A third of them from Him, causing a heavy toll.
I, the mighty one, who has devastated civilizations and old cultures,
I, the greatest tempter and seducer of all time that joyfully tortures
Human beings and God alike, for whom man is nothing but a mere toy,
Is it hard for me to seduce Adam and Eve who're only a girl and a boy?
I'll go and get the woman, and she will get me the man.
No wonder God called her "woman," she is "woe-man!"

No problem friends, it's easy, a piece of cake rather.
If I can get one now, I will surely get later the other.
Even as I have destructed many families in the past,
I'll destroy theirs too. And theirs won't be the last.
You all know my style—to get the husband, I get his wife first.
If I don't get her, I change my tactics, and scheme the worst—
I get the children, and through them, I get papa and mama,
Dismantling the whole family, putting them all in dilemma.
So, let me go get little Eve, and she'll get me bulky Adam.
Otherwise, I am no more Lucifer. Otherwise, I am sham!

AZAZEL
Eh! You're so full of yourself, Satan. I can't stand your attitude!
Didn't we all participate in all of these? Where's your gratitude?

Semazya and Annanel node their heads in agreement with Azazel.

LUCIFER
(bowing before Azazel in mockery)
Oh, yeah, your excellency, the little, tough devil,
Without whose help I could not have done evil.
(back to himself)
But the truth is that, I, Lucifer, the morning star, tread on fire,
Yet, fire doesn't burn me! I burn it! I consume it! I never retire
Until the day when I'll be dumped in that Lake of Fire.
Then, we'll see who'll burn who. Until that time I aspire
To mess up God's plan by traveling across the Universe;
Yes indeed, hopping from one world to another to traverse
Distances nobody would ever dare dream to cover,
Faster than the twinkling of a star, without endeavor.

Yeah! My anger is lightening, my burping thunder.
I grab the sun with my hands and tear it asunder.
I sweep away the stars with a little broom.
The sky is my bed, the earth my bathroom.
I, Lucifer, the contender of God, shooting stars are my shower.
True, I'm fallen from heaven and grace, but never from power!

ANNANEL
(disgusted with Lucifer's bragging)
Hey Satan, who're you talking to? Your bragging is old and dusty!
Don't you have anything better to say? Where's your modesty?

SEMAZYA
What for is this self-aggrandizement
Satan? Is it your ego's appeasement?

Lucifer ignores his lieutenants and continues to talk to himself.

LUCIFER
Since knowledge and power are unquenchable drinks,
In order to pursue and acquire them, man sinks and sinks
Into the darker depths, forgetful of the consequence
Of flirting with me, which to God, is a grand offence.
So I entice curious and megalomaniac man with false promises
Of unattainable knowledge and power, until he foolishly misses

The point and dabbles, making it very easy for me to submerge him
Into a bottomless abyss, when he is unsuspecting, thinking he's trim.
When God gives man scriptures and golden rules by which to abide,
I shove down his throat misleading, demonic books so that he'd hide
And stray from God in confusion, and indulge naively in the occult,
To be cut off from God, entrapped in my world of darkness and cult
Where he'll never ever rise again once he violently trips,
And no force whatsoever will free him from my grips.
What's the so-called extra-perception,
But an exposition to my deception?
What's knowledge of witchcraft and the occult,
But marriage with me to worship me in my cult?
And what, in reality, is its end-result,
But hell to face my torment and insult?

I've advantage over man—I'm millions of years older in age.
As such, he can't be my match in experience and knowledge.
Besides, I see him clearly and read his mind and heart,
But he can't see me. I'm invisible to him, be he smart
Or dumb. It's even better for me when he foolishly denies
My existence. I'll influence him behind the scene till he dies.
In a way, it's very good that man is dumb and ignorant of my existence—
If he knows I exist, he'll know God too, exists, being logically persistence.
Still, I'm sick and tired of men's excuses for their actions. They blame
Me for everything they do wrongly by giving unfairly all kinds of lame
Excuses, instead of being responsible. I can never burn them aflame
Unless they're willing to be flammable. Man opens his heart's door,
And I enter. Some even adore me, forgetting it's God they should adore.
Man is engaged in making ends meet and easing the burden of his life.
I've nothing to do except unleashing on him tirelessly havoc and strife.
Yes, yes! I'm jealous that God appointed man to rule the planet,
Controlling nature, drawing all animals to himself like a magnet,
Reigning over Earth forever, establishing a dynasty,
Being almost equal to God in splendor and majesty.
Oh, no! I won't allow this! I'll mislead man to forfeit
His rights to me, and I'll rule the world by counterfeit!

SEMAZYA
(mockingly)
Your ambition is limitless, but great is your loss.

AZAZEL
Semazya, that's viciously gross!
Remember he's still your boss.

LUCIFER
(shunning the two)
God created man in His image, but man is the contrary—
As stupid and as crazy as us, instead of being exemplary.
Sitting on a branch of God's tree, enjoying frantically its delicious fruit,
He tries to cut the branch he's sitting on and wishes the tree to uproot.
The pattern is the same in every age and every civilization—
Man is blinded by materialism, lacking spiritual realization.
He's immersed in the stinky pool of sexual immorality, perversion,
Avariciousness, war-mongering, exploitation of the weak, diversion,
Godlessness, blood-shedding, deception, lawlessness, domination,
Havoc, turmoil, hate, covetousness, betrayal, and self-extermination.
That is how human history was. That's how human history
Will be, till I'm cast into the Lake of Fire, losing my victory.
Created in the image of God, breathing God's breath, man negates
God's existence. He'll know God only when he enters hell's gates.
Most humans are evil and rebellious as I am, by nature,
And I'll confirm this truth with my authentic signature.

SEMAZYA
No matter what, God loves man. Lucifer, stop being jealous!
Control yourself, boss. You'll hurt, unless you become callous . . .

Eve appears on the scene to check the Tree of Knowledge. The fallen angels are invisible to her. They wonder why she is there.

LUCIFER
(crossing his index fingers on his lips)
Hush! . . . Look, Eve's here!
Wow! She displays no fear!

ANGLE ON EVE.

Eve stares at the Tree of Knowledge with a desire to touch and eat it.

EVE
You draw me to yourself again and again, you Tree of Knowledge!
I'm totally enamored and possessed by you, I should acknowledge!
O, forbidden fruit, you're so gorgeous, unlike any! You don't seem
A killer to me. How can a charming one like you kill? I can't deem
You to be a killer . . . And why should knowledge lead
To death? Is knowledge terrible? Isn't it a great need? . . .
O, Tree of Knowledge! Aren't you really too beautiful and too attractive
To be a killer? How can you hide death in your beauty? I'm very reactive

And responsive to your charm, though you don't speak to me.
Would you really kill me? Tell me, are you really my enemy?

(pause)

God said you're absolutely free to eat the fruits of every tree,
Except the one in the middle of the garden. If so, am I free
Absolutely? I'm not absolutely free as I can't eat of every tree.
I'm a mere creature. Only God the Creator is absolutely free.
However big I think of myself, I made neither my body nor my soul.
I created none of myself. Nor was I able to decide to be short or tall.
As I woke up from non-existence, I found my body and soul. That's all.
The very fruits that sustain my body weren't made by me. I can't even
Grow plants, let alone create seeds. It's God that even waters my garden.

(pause)

Nevertheless, is God Himself free absolutely?
Can God really do whatever He likes completely?
Since He's indestructible, can He destruct
Himself if he wishes and then reconstruct?
What's His weak point? Can He hate if He wishes to hate?
Can He contradict His divine nature and emotional state?
No. I don't think He can. So, God too, has His limitations.
No wonder we have restrictions, as we are His imitations.

(pause)

Restriction . . . freedom's greatest enemy, O, restriction!
You're creating between me and my God a big friction . . .

LUCIFER
(knowing full well that Eve doesn't hear him)
Oh no, Eve, restriction is the friend of freedom. It is a bridle
That restrains it from galloping into a cliff. I so riddle the riddle.

EVE
God said, don't go even close to it because it is close,
Indeed mysterious, closed to me. It can cause my loss.
It's even untouchable, let alone to be eatable. What sort of power
Does it possess that prevents us from touching it? It does tower
Higher than all the trees of the Garden of Eden
And higher than myself and my husband even

In its awesome power. The other trees are easy to get.
The other trees aren't scary. Once I taste them, I forget
About them. This one is so hallowed and so sacred as if it's holy.
I've to admit it's stronger than me. I adore and dread it wholly.

(pause)

But then, is it really stronger than myself? Was I not formed
In God's image? No, I'm stronger, though I get weak stormed
By its beauty and tempting power. The decision to eat of it or not
Is surely controlled by me and not by this tree located in this spot.
I have free will. It can't put its fruits in my mouth forcefully.
Let me touch it and see what it'll do to me. I'm in control fully.

She touches some of the fruits that are hanging on a branch within her reach, breaking God's commandment not to go near it, let alone touch it. Lucifer and his angels watch her in disbelief and shock at her audacity. The touch of the untouchable sends a shiver and a spasm through her. She gets goose bumps. She plucks some of the magical fruits and stares at them daringly and defiantly.

Not only I touched you, I can also squeeze you, holding you in my palm.
Yes, I desire to devour you frantically, whatever happens. I am so calm.
I'm in control . . . you tiny, alluring fruits, would you really kill me if I ate
You up now . . . Perhaps you would. Perhaps I should eat you at a later date . . .
I wish my eating you had no everlasting consequence. God promised
I will fill the earth with my children. How can this be? Have I missed
Some of his prophecies? How can I have children if I die? Did He imply
I will live long and die? If so, will I pass on my curse? Does it apply
To my children? Will they too, be cursed like me and die? Will the whole
World be cursed through me? If so, we will all fall into a bottomless hole!

(pause)

But I feel like eating you, to uncover your secret!

She brings the fruits near her mouth. Her saliva drips . . . she eyes the fruits for a moment with a strong desire to eat them. She then changes her mind.

I won't eat you now! You see, I'm tougher than you, though I fret . . .

She squeezes the fruits in her palms, throws them away, smells with relish the juice that has smeared her palm, and runs to her house speedily.

TWO SHOTS:

Lucifer and Semazya express their reaction.

LUCIFER
Ah, friends, we missed a big, big chance!

SEMAZYA
Thinking she was going to eat them, I was ready to dance.

LUCIFER
She's very daring . . . She challenged God. Rest assured, I will make
Her eat them sooner or later. Her husband, too, will eat for her sake.

FADE OUT.

FADE IN:

EXT. NEAR THE HOUSE OF ADAM AND EVE. AFTERNOON.

After Adam and Eve live in Paradise for seven years, according to God's heavenly time, which is two million, five hundred and fifty-five thousand years in human, earthly time, resisting temptation, worshiping God and observing His Commandment, Lucifer and his angels scout around their house and see that Eve is alone. They move towards the house. Archangel Phanuel, the guardian angel of Adam and Eve, tries to stop them from tempting and misleading her.

LUCIFER
(to his angels)
Let's go get that little girl and fall her down on the ground,
If that gardener or farmer husband of hers is not around!

PHANUEL
(confronting Lucifer)
Don't you ever hope
To tempt Eve. Stop!
If you have the guts, you accursed tempter,
Tempt her when her husband comes later!

LUCIFER
When the front door is open no more,
I've to get in through the back door.

Raguel flies in to interfere.

RAGUEL
(to Phanuel)
Adam was tempted but prevailed, for sure.
It's Eve's turn to be tempted and endure.

PHANUEL
(to Lucifer)
Are you going to be a raven again
To deceive Eve and inflict pain?

LUCIFER
I'll choose whatever stratagem suits my needs.
I share with none my evil schemes and deeds.

Lucifer changes himself into a SNAKE and approaches Eve at the front yard of her house where she is tending her flowers.

ANGLE ON EVE.

In her solitude, she questions why God created her, and why Adam and herself are different. .

EVE
While I appreciate the fact
God created me, His act
Of creation, however, is an exercise of his fantasy
Which Gave Him immense joy, thrill, and ecstasy.
God did not consult with me on that particular spot
And day, whether I wanted to be created or not.
Truly, I had no say in this matter to object
Or approve it. Which means I am an object
Of God...Am I an object of his love, really?
Maybe... If it is so, why am I talking silly?...

Why did God make Adam and me different?
Why is he male, and I female? Why inherent
In us are different emotions? I've inside me a superb womb to bear
Children. There's no life-nurturing womb in him. Unlike him, I wear
No beard. Adam has no breasts. His wide chest is like a plain field.
My chest is like two hills. He secretes sperm. It's eggs that I yield.
His voice is coarse and low, but my voice is softer and higher,
When our voices mix, they make a sweet and resonating choir.
I'm drawn to him, and he to me. We attract each other because
We're unlike. For creating our attraction, we've God to applause.
I'm like soil in which grow plants, though I haven't grown any.
Adam's like a seed-sower . . . God said my children will be many.
I've my own seeds that mix with his to help them sprout, even as soil
Has in it rich minerals that nourish seeds, which otherwise would spoil.
If I'm soil in which grows life, I must be very important.
Without me, Adam cannot do much, even for an instant.
This holds true for me too, though I feel to be important.
We need each other. In fact, I need him every instant.
He has lived in this Garden when he was the only
One. I need company. I can't imagine being lonely.

LUCIFER
(interrupting her thinking)
Peace be unto you, Eve, where's your husband? You feel lonely?

EVE
What a question? Of course I feel lonely when I'm the only
Woman in this vast Garden. How about you, lovely snake?

LUCIFER
I, too, am lonely . . . just dropped in to break
Your solitude actually by talking
To you, when I saw you walking . . .
Has your husband gone far or is he around?

EVE
He has gone far . . . eastbound.

LUCIFER
Before you were made out of his ribs he used
To play with me every day. In fact, he amused
Himself in my company, but unfortunately, he forgot
About me totally and squarely, Eve, as soon as he got
You in this place and garden.

EVE
Oh, really? . . . I'm so sorry . . . I beg your pardon . . .

LUCIFER
Not only you took my place,
Dear Eve, but even my space.

EVE
(feeling guilty)
I'm so sorry . . .

LUCIFER
Please don't worry,
This is an old story.
Adam used to pet and pet me daily and spoil
Me. He liked me so much he allowed me to coil
Around his body, absolutely unconcerned I'd soil
Him. Oh, how he enjoyed my soft touch!
I was his only pet and companion, as such!
I really was his joy's peak.
I was his brat, so to speak.

EVE
Is that right? Come up from the ground.
I too, want to feel your touch. Coil around
Me. Since you're flexible, elastic, and slender,
Oh sweet thing, you must be soft and tender.

Lucifer hisses and slowly climbs up her right leg and coils around her body.

LUCIFER
Oh, delicious Eve, you're as soft as feather.
And your fragrance is lovelier than heather.
Your skin's as soothing as the petals of the lavender,
It's so smooth like a babe, so slippery and so tender.
How lucky are Adam's arms, which embrace
You, and his eyes, which see your radiant face!

EVE
O! you beautiful snake, you're full of charm and wit.
Frankly, I'm flattered! You're really sweet every bit!
By making me feel gay,
You just made my day!

AZAZEL
Wow! He already got her!

SEMAZYA
He's acting like a lover!

ANNANEL
He put her in his armpit without much endeavor!

LUCIFER
(coiling around her hips)
More comfortable than horseback are your bow-like hips.
Oh, such budding lips! Would that I kiss your popping lips!

EVE
(naively)
Why not, if you like them that much?

LUCIFER
Oh, Eve, I love them a whole bunch!

He kisses her lips and continues to hiss . . .

EVE
You're so romantic! You really know how to kiss!

LUCIFER
You bet, my darling. Just because I hiss,
Doesn't mean I don't know how to kiss.

185

EVE
How did you learn to kiss?

LUCIFER
Oh, it comes natural . . . it's a heavenly bliss.

EVE
Adam has never kissed me like this.

LUCIFER
I told you, your poor Adam's just a little boy
Who doesn't know how his woman to enjoy . . .
There's a secret that pains me that I should reveal
To you, Eve. If I told you what it is, maybe I can heal.

EVE
What? Secret that pains you?
Reveal it to me now . . . please do!

LUCIFER
When I tell you this, please don't get angry or fret—
I've always admired you and loved you in secret.

EVE
(surprised and laughing)
You love me? . . . Ha! Ha! Ha! . . . But you're not a man!
How on earth can a small snake like you love a woman?

LUCIFER
Oh, how I envy Adam! I'd have contested
With him if I were a man really, and tested
His bravery. It's to avoid this sort of rivalry God put only
One impotent man in this garden, making you so lonely.

Lucifer coils around her neck.

EVE
Oh, you're something, snake! . . .
Ah! It's tight! Get off my neck!

Lucifer leaves her neck, moves to her chest, and presses on her breasts.

I feel good on my chest where your belly rests.
Little snake, are you now fondling my breasts?

LUCIFER
Yes, I am.

EVE
(sternly)
Don't! My breasts are reserved for Adam!

LUCIFER
How about your rosy lips,
And your bow-like hips?
Believe me, Adam is an inexperienced boy,
Who doesn't know how a woman to enjoy.

EVE
Are you really older than Adam?

LUCIFER
I was created before he was molded. Yes, I am!

EVE
Molded? . . . Hmm . . . you mean formed?

LUCIFER
(with laughter)
I mean deformed . . .
Eve, you should be informed—
Do you know you're better than Adam?

EVE
I am?

LUCIFER
Adam was deformed from very cheap dirt, in a crib.
But you, my gash! You were created from a fine rib.
Therefore, you're higher in quality.
He doesn't share with you equality.

EVE
(raising her eyebrows)
Really? I didn't know that part.

LUCIFER
So, you're supposed to be more smart.
You should lead him actually.
He should follow you, factually.
By the way, are you happily married to Adam?

EVE
Yes, I am.

LUCIFER
Since you, Eve, are of much higher breed
Than Adam, carrying in you the best seed,
You should lead, and Adam should follow,
However hard he finds this fact to swallow.

EVE
An interesting idea, though doubtful if it's true, O! Snake.

LUCIFER
It's true, believe me, my love. It's as true as I'm not fake!

EVE
I'll think about what you said. I need time.

LUCIFER
The day you take action, you'll be prime.
My advice to you is act more, think less.
Too much thinking renders action useless.

EVE
I wonder how all the animals we rule can easily talk
To humans; even as easily as they creep, fly, or walk.

LUCIFER
Now man has ability to converse with us at the most,
If man abuses evilly our trust and us, it will be lost.

EVE
Oh, charming snake, you do speak so eloquently.
I don't come across animals like you frequently.
You also exhibit intelligence of a higher degree.
You are extremely intriguing. Do you agree?
In fact, you sound like an old sage.
I'm curious—what's your exact age?

LUCIFER
Oh, little girl, Oh, my sweetie, Oh, young Eve,
I'm much, much older than you can perceive.
I was alive long before Earth was conceived;
Before even her intricate fibers were weaved.

Much older than the Universe, I'm from a long time ago.
I've seen great civilizations and populations come and go.
Admirable man reaches a peak and tumbles down. He's done.
And then, he rises and starts all over again from square one.

Millions of years ago, I rode on the back of the Behemoth.
I also flew and soared with them high. It was in the remote
Past. Most of all, from horizon to horizon, brightening
The sky, I rode like a horse both thunder and lightning.
I was so glorious and awesome, dear Eve,
Beyond what you can imagine and conceive.
In those days, even angels bowed to me in reverence.
In spite of difficulties, I've survived in perseverance.

EVE
(amused, but suspiciously)
People lived in the past? Give me a break!
I find what you say hard to imagine, snake.

LUCIFER
You're naïve,
My dear Eve.
You think you two are the first humans that have ever lived?
Puff! You're full of yourselves! Now this makes me aggrieved.
Peoples with higher civilizations and refined cultures
Have lived for ages, forming complex social structures.

EVE
Where on earth are they, dear snake? I know that at least,
In this garden, my husband and I exist with many a beast.

LUCIFER
Don't you believe me? Why would I tell you lies.
I'm talking about Earth, and not this Paradise.
But the peoples on Earth vanished because of decay.

AZAZEL
(to himself in a low voice)
You're lying, Lucifer. It's because they followed your way!

LUCIFER
But their remnants exist to this day.

EVE
Really? Where? I'm ignorant . . . I beg your pardon.

LUCIFER
O, girl, the world is much bigger than this garden.
Yes, yes, you're right in saying you're ignorant.
There's a lot you don't know. God didn't grant
You knowledge. That's why He threateningly said:
"If you eat of the Tree of Knowledge, you'll be dead!"

Eve blinks her eyes, puzzled by his remarks.

LUCIFER
(contd.)
Can I ask you a question, if you don't mind?
Please tell me why you are spiritually blind.

EVE
What do you mean? You're confusing my mind.

LUCIFER
Did God really permit you to eat of the fruits of every tree?
In other words, to eat the fruits of every tree, are you free?

EVE
Yes, except one tree, we're free
To eat the fruits of every tree.

LUCIFER
Oh, miserable Eve, then you're not really free,
If you're forbidden to eat the fruits of every tree.

EVE
Oh, my! I too, have thought of it in those terms.
O! Snake, your words have some truthful germs.

LUCIFER
(giggling)
Germs? Ha, ha, ha! Indeed germs!
I like it when you talk in witty terms.
Let me tell you something, which blows away your mind—
There are things you ought to know, lest you lag behind.
There were real men and civilizations that invented machines.
They were technologically and scientifically advanced nations.

In those days, intelligent men were able to fly
Wherever they chose to, dominating the sky.
They flew from one galaxy to another in an instant.
They traveled to and from planets far and distant.

Being in one country, conquering totally time and space,
They were able to talk with someone in a very far place.
Sitting in their living room in front of a screen,
They could see remote visions they had never seen
Controlling what they see with a remote control,
Because knowledge played in their lives a big role.

EVE
You're blowing away my mind, genius snake!
I don't get it; but am listening. Am fully awake!
How did they do that . . . I'm struggling
To understand . . . This is mind boggling . . .

LUCIFER
Those extraordinary people had a secret knowledge,
Which sharpened their minds like a knife's edge!
Sadly, they lost it all and suffered a tremendous pain.
It'll take thousands of years to reach that level again.

EVE
You said they had a secret knowledge. What kind
Of knowledge would actually sharpen the mind?

LUCIFER
They ate the fruits of a fantastic tree, which was hidden.

EVE
Could it be the Tree of Knowledge God has forbidden?

LUCIFER
Did God really say of that tree you shall not eat even a bit?

EVE
Yes He did. We'll die for sure, if we eat even a bit. That's it!

LUCIFER
(pretending he doesn't know)
Hmm! That's interesting .Which one exactly is it, in this wood?

EVE
It's the one in the middle. It reveals the evil and the good.

LUCIFER
Well, those people who were flying machines in the skies
Did eat the magic fruits, which opened their spiritual eyes.

EVE
That's amazing! But too bad it will kill!

LUCIFER
Are you kidding! On the contrary, it will heal... Yes it will!

EVE
God said, we'll die the day we eat of that tree!

LUCIFER
Oh, no! I don't totally agree!
The day you eat of that tree,
You'll be completely wise and free.
In fact, you'll know everything God knows,
Because that tree opens your eyes and shows
You everything God has secretly hidden
From your views. That's why it's forbidden.
Yeah! God doesn't want you to be His equal,
Which's why He says that, that tree is unusual.
Believe me, honey, if you eat of that sweet and fantastic tree,
You'll yourself be god surely, omnipotent, everlasting, and free!

ANGLE ON ANNANEL, AZAZEL AND SEMAZYA.

ANNANEL
Now he set her up, without leaving any gap!

AZAZEL
Yeah! There's no way out now. She's in his trap!

SEMAZYA
He knows how to wrap the truth with falsehood's wrap!

EVE
(shocked and surprised)
Is that right? I thought God was on our side!

LUCIFER
Oh, no . . . if He was so, why would He hide
The secret of this hallucinogenic plant,
Making it so untouchable and so scant?
Trust me, my love, you'll never ever die if you eat
Of it. In fact, you'll feel a surge of energy and heat,
Vigor and stamina, and achieve divine quality,
Sharing with God Almighty absolute equality,
Enjoying knowledge of the occult with such vitality,
Thus attaining even as God, ultimate immortality . . .
Therefore, beloved Eve, be bold, do not hesitate—
Eat of that Knowledge Tree, because, if you ate
Of that powerful, delicious fruit, with certainty,
You'd be a goddess, attaining wisdom and deity.

EVE
(impressed much)
Yeah, I want to know everything God knows,
And see every hidden thing this Tree shows.
But I need to think . . . I need time . . .

LUCIFER
The moment you take action, you'll be prime.
Like I said before, act more and think less—
Too much thinking renders action useless.

Lucifer moves away from her and watches her.

ANGLE ON ARCHANGELS PHANUEL AND RAGUEL.

PHANUEL
(sadly)
I wonder how she could easily be hooked and fished.

RAGUEL
What a tragedy! That's it! She's finished!

ANGLE ON AZAZEL

AZAZEL
He made it! He led her into his trap!

SEMAZYA
(clapping)
Let's applaud Lucifer! Let's clap!

The three fallen angels clap.

EVE
(to herself)
The snake said, "Act more and think less,
"Too much thinking renders action useless."
Oh, how true it is! How clever!
Is this animal honest, however? . . .

Is it deceiving me? But it's only a beautiful serpent.
It's not one of the fallen angels who'd never repent . . .
It's a poor, innocent little being opening my eyes and ears
To help me liberate myself to conquer my haunting fears,
Waking me up from a numbing spiritual slumber,
Trying to show me good things in greater number.
God said we'll die if we know even for an instance.
I would rather know and die than live in ignorance!
I am more daring than my hesitant husband, more adventure-
Seeking and curious. Maybe, this is a woman's trait or nature.

LUCIFER
Oh, yeah! Right on, sweetie!
You're now becoming witty!

Eve goes to the forbidden tree. Lucifer, as well as God's and Lucifer's angels, follow her.

EVE
Because it is forbidden, it arouses my curiosity.
Must be very tasty, capable of making one witty.
Oh, knowledge! Oh, tempting curiosity!
If I act foolishly without thinking, I'd wish rather to take it back.
Since I'm calculating the risk involved, I won't be taken aback!
I think it's about time to taste
This ever-tempting tree in haste,
Lest I waver and change my mind
And remain indefinitely blind!
(looking at the forbidden tree)
Ah! You enchanting and alluring Tree of Knowledge
That can deliver me out of ignorance, if I acknowledge!
You've been violently tempting me all my age.
Today, I'll have you, and be like God, a sage!
And once I am a God, I don't have to obey God, since
I'll be His equal. So, I've to eat the fruit by all means!

I understand profoundly: to know or not to know, to live in ignorance
Or to die in knowledge is the question. I choose over eternal endurance
Pure, mind-sharpening knowledge even if I succeed to obtain
It only for a short moment! I wouldn't mind dying to attain
It, if knowledge leads to death indeed. I've decided, I'll not retreat!
You wonderful Tree of Knowledge. I'll relish you! I'll have a treat!
I am a woman—once determined, I can't shamelessly backslide.
Let me rush forward—I, Eve, have no fear whatsoever if I collide!

She runs towards the Forbidden Tree like a mad dog and bumps into it. She talks to the tree, looking upward.

PHANUEL
Ah! . . . I wish I could stop her from eating of that tree!

RAGUEL
You can guard her but can't interfere in her will. She's free.
Even God wouldn't interfere in her freewill.
Yes, she has freewill to change her mind still.

EVE
Oh! You intriguing, magical tree! You're distinct, yet misty!
How long do you tempt me, arousing my feminine curiosity!
How long are you going to be shrouded in mystery!
I'll unveil your secrets right now and make history!

LUCIFER
(to himself)
Indeed, my bold rebel, you'll make history; and you'll plunge, no doubt,
Your children, into a bottomless abyss of which they'll never come out!

EVE
(hesitating)
Caught between reason and emotion, snared by desire and temptation,
To die or not to die is the question. I'm trapped by endless hesitation.
Worst than my own personal death is my fear of its implication—
Will I really cause my children to die? Ah, such a complication!
However much I reason, I know one thing with precision—
The future of my children depends on my present decision . . .
Oh, no, no! I shouldn't be unconcerned. I shouldn't dare
Ruin their future. I've an immense responsibility to bear.
Yes indeed, my responsibility is huge. I should not rush
To eat these awesome fruits frantically. What if I brush
Myself against death actually? I've to think. What if I really
Die? What will become of me then? God created me freely;

That's true. And yet, I know I am not absolutely free—
I'll suffer the consequence of eating from this tree.
Real freedom is the liberty to do anything, anywhere, in essence,
Without being tormented with guilt and suffering the consequence.

(pause)

Yes, I think I shouldn't flirt
With death . . . I've to be alert . . .

She retreats from the tree. Lucifer advances towards her.

LUCIFER
Do it, Eve! A woman doesn't backslide, right? Don't chicken
Out! Aren't you brave? I'm disappointed and grief-stricken!...

EVE
Listen, snake, I don't know what's to be dead actually.
Therefore, I don't want to flirt with death, factually.

LUCIFER
Dying is nothing but being exposed to a hidden reality, virtually.
A fantastic and superb reality will unfold before you, as I said,
If you eat the fruits. I can get them for you, if you seek my aid.

EVE
(attracted by the idea of a new reality)
The idea of being exposed to a new reality is intriguing . . .
I want to see the new reality, but indecision is fatiguing . . .
God said clearly we'll be cut off from Him if we ate of it.
He forbade us to taste of the Tree of Knowledge, even a bit.
What it means to be really cut off from Him, I've no clue;
Even as I've no clue why the tree is green and the sky blue.

LUCIFER
To be cut off from God means to be set loose and free
From His grip. Be resolute! Eat of this fantastic tree!
Remember what I said, "Act more and think less,
"For too much thinking renders action useless."
Moreover, as you said, a woman is more daring. I'll congratulate
You when you take the fruits boldly. Be brave! Don't capitulate!

EVE
Hesitation is very bad . . . I'll take action. Yes, I will break
God's commandment . . . You're so right, O! lovely snake!

196

Eve eats the forbidden fruits. The fallen angels leap up with immense joy! The good angels grieve.

EVE
(relishing the forbidden fruits)
Oh, it's yummy! It's so delicious!
But why did God say it's vicious? . . .

PHANUEL
Yuck! . . . No! No! No! No!

RAGUEL
I never imagined she would do so!

PHANUEL
I hope Adam won't take
It for his wife's sake.
If he takes it convinced by her, his ties with God will break,
He'll surely be immersed in sin, and his life will be at stake.

Lucifer gets closer to Eve, still disguised as a snake.

LUCIFER
You've now become more rebellious and ambitious
Than me, oh, defiant woman, in fact, more vicious!
Do you see anything, Eve? Look around.

The fallen angels manifest themselves to her. The sound of weird music is heard.

EVE
(looking around)
Oh, my! I see strange angels, and I hear a weird sound!

LUCIFER
(laughing sarcastically)
I told you a lot would happen
When your eyes and ears open.

AZAZEL
(laughing hysterically)
Welcome, my defiant comrade, to the world of sorcery and witchcraft!
I'm the famous and illustrious Azazel. I possess craft and spell. I draft
Evil and implement it swiftly. I'm more piercing than spear and draft.

LUCIFER
He's God's most trusted servant.
Certainly, he's savant and fervent.
Listen now carefully if he has anything to say.
Don't say nay to him. Simply say, "Okay! Okay!"
Also, listen to the sound of music, which can heal you if you're sick,
Which's so haunting and so mystic. This is all real and not any trick.

AZAZEL
Hey, Eve! You now see what God sees.
Thank the snake kneeling on your knees.

EVE
(kneeling down before Lucifer)
I'm like God! I love all these angels that are smiling
To me. Thank you, snake, and you angels for piling
All these mesmerizing layers of beauty around
Me and for this sweet, haunting, musical sound.

LUCIFER
O, naive Eve, do kneel down for me like that! I'm exhilarated!
This, only this, has been my dream ever since I've been created!

AZAZEL
Dear Eve, if you really love your stubborn husband and care
For him, encourage him to do what you did. Make him aware
Of the immense beauty, charm, and captivating magic
That encompass you . . . yeah, convince him with logic.

EVE
I will surely convince him to take
Some of the fruits I took, to make
His day, like the snake made my day.
I'm sure my husband won't say, "Nay."

Adam appears on the scene.

ANGLE ON ADAM.

Lucifer hides right away.

ADAM
Hello, the apple of my eye! You missed me when I was away?

EVE
Yes and no, because the beautiful snake made my day.

ADAM
The snake? How?

EVE
(looking around)
It was here. I don't know where it is now.
It told me the forbidden tree is best for acquiring knowledge.
I ate it. Oh, it's so delicious! The snake's right, I acknowledge.
I now know things, which only God knows.
Adam, my love, I see amazing scenes: rows
Of angels, flowers, animals, rivers, mountains, and skies.
I hear sweet music, voices, sounds, and even haunting cries.
It's quite exciting, darling, a hidden reality is unfolding
Right in front of me. I'm glued to it! It's really holding
My utmost attention. I wish you can experience
The same. It's raising the level of my conscience.
I've transcended you. I've extra perceptive power and an altered state
Of consciousness. I listen only to whatever my heart and head dictate.

ADAM
(shouting, utterly shocked)
No way, Eve! Did you eat really what God said you shall not eat!
Oh, no! No! . . . Ah! I'm shocked! I'm stricken by a wave of heat!
You're going to die now! That's your end!
God's law is firm! God's law won't bend!

EVE
(calmly, with sweet voice)
Look, I'm still alive,
In fact, I do thrive!...
Adam, my mother and husband, the flesh of my flesh, don't be dummy—
What's life without me? Won't you die with me, since you love me?
O! Adam, the pupil of my eye, the bone of my bone,
If I die, would you really live for eternity all alone?

ADAM
(softened)
You know for sure, that I love you, my dear Eve;
I also love my God, who wants me forever to live.

EVE
Adam, do you know why God actually forbade
Us to eat the fruits? Do you really know He made
That tree exceptional, so that, in actuality,
Only He could have access to this secret reality
Which's unfolding, and I'm accessing right now, as we speak?
I now know a bit of what God knows, having reached a peak!

Lucifer, who is now in his real self, grins and approaches Eve, being visible only to her.

LUCIFER
Yes, honey, you're now yourself a god,
Because you defied what God forebode.
Tell your foolish husband to be bold and wise
Like you. Threaten you'll leave him otherwise.

EVE
(wondering who is talking to her)
Sure, I will!... So, my beloved Adam, please trust me. Feel free
And be like God by eating of that phenomenal Knowledge Tree.
Moreover, if you do love me as you say, do what I've done.
Or else, since you've not risen to my level, I've to abandon
You, if not physically, at least emotionally and mentally.
Rest assured, we'll never understand each other totally.

ADAM
Eve, loving, I love you, but I love God too.
I should obey Him as much as I love you.

EVE
Then, you'll lose me for good!

ADAM
I had lived alone before you joined me in this wood!

LUCIFER
(to Eve)
Remember you've a slice of honey between your thighs?
Tell him firmly he won't have it if he cries or even dies,
Unless and until
He bends to your will.
Use all your feminine beauty and power, Eve, to dominate
The conversation. Persuade him till your ideas germinate
In his head. Weaken his strong will with your soft voice
Till he completely surrenders, and is left without a choice.

Once you've done this, on top of this, and apart
From this, touch his tenderness to move his heart—
Pull your hair, rave, moan, and wail, applying any sort
Of gimmick. Use your feminine jewel-tears as a last resort.

EVE
(to Adam)
Then I won't give you any more that slice
Of sweet thing you love between my thighs.

ADAM
(shocked)
No, you won't do that! You know the joy it can bring!
There's no way I can live without that delicious thing!
You see love, there's nothing in this entire garden sweeter
Than that nectar between your thighs. Everything else's bitter.

EVE
Then do what I did, boldly defying death, and rise to my level!
Be decisive and know everything I know about good and evil!

ADAM
(after hesitation)
Be it! You're the flesh of my flesh,
I'll share your fate, and if I enmesh
Myself hurtfully as a result of this, it's that,
My sweet, I treasure you a lot. Come what
May, I will not oppose you and go my own way.
Whatever the consequence, I'll do what you say.
Moreover, Sweet Eve, I admit that I'm dying to know
What you and God know, and in that knowledge grow.
Not only grow in that knowledge, but I want also to glow.

EVE
Then eat it quickly! Yes, don't be hesitant or slow!

Adam plucks the fruits and holds them with his left hand. He looks at them indecisively for a moment. His hand shakes. He sweats profusely.

ADAM
O, Forbidden Tree that reveals the good and evil, planted by God to test
Me and my wife, why do you mesmerize me so? It seems that I can't rest
Until I taste you like my bold wife did. Yet, if I ate you, the repercussion
Would tantalize my soul. This is a very sensitive issue unfit for discussion

With God. He said the impact of eating it will affect the yet-to-be-born
Children of mine. But why should they die because of me and be torn
Apart from God forevermore? That'll be selfish of me. Flirting
With you is flirting with death and sin, which would be hurting
My standing with my Creator. Is knowledge really worth dying for?

EVE
Yes, it is! Only it, makes us like God. Eat it quickly, therefore!

ADAM
No, Eve! I hesitate to eat it. I'm fear-stricken! The consequence is grave.
Let me remain ignorant than suffer the consequence feigning I'm brave.

He retreats from the tree and deliberates in his mind for a moment:

Now faced to choose between my wife and my Maker,
Should I choose my wife, because she's my caretaker?
In truth, the partner of my lonely life is my wife,
God's in His holy abode. He's not always in my life.
What's the point of losing my wife to maintain
A garden? This will be a total lose, not a gain...
But then it's not all about loss or gain of a garden,
It's about a rebellion against God. Will God pardon
Me really after I betray Him? Will my Maker
Forgive me after sinning to keep my caretaker?
Oh, what shall I do? I'm torn between my wife
And my God, and between death and eternal life...
My wife ate the forbidden fruits; yet is alive.
God said we will die, but she does still strive
To live forevermore. Is God a liar? In a way, I admire
My wife's guts...O, what's going on! I'm in quagmire!
Why is my wife alive? Is she going to die later on?
Oh, I don't want to live alone,
After the flesh of my flesh, the bone
Of my bone, is lost and forever gone!...
O, I don't know what to do! I really don't know how
To take all this! O, my God, come and help me now!

Eve, Lucifer, and his lieutenants get disappointed that Adam is hesitating to eat the fruits.

EVE
Adam, I thought you had some burning fire in your guts!
If you don't eat these fruits, go crunch your tasteless nuts!
I can't believe you're so hesitant and cowardly, Adam!
If you're a man worth your balls, now be decisive. I am
Brave though I am a woman. Be brave as I am, Adam!

LUCIFER
That's the way to talk to this wimp, madam.
Believe me, Eve, not only he doesn't have the guts,
But even the balls. His balls are smaller than nuts.

ADAM
If it was just dying for you alone, I'll. But, Eve, I don't want to pass death
On to my children. God will punish me, instead of giving me flower wreath.

EVE
You talk about children as if you have any.

ADAM
But God said, you and I will have many.

EVE
What's the use of having ignorant children who live forevermore?
We need illuminated ones who'd unlock knowledge's closed door.

ADAM
I'm sorry. I'll do anything for you except eating of this tree, dear wife.
This is a matter of life and death. No! I don't want to lose eternal life.

EVE
You may gain eternal life, but you'll lose me forever!

ADAM
(broken by fear of losing Eve)
No, I don't want to lose you either, Eve! Never!

He embraces her tightly. She gets out of his arms forcefully and retreats from him. He is confused, sad, and in dilemma. He breathes heavily. He looks at the Tree of Knowledge hatefully. He gets angry at God for creating the Tree of Knowledge of the good and evil.

EVE
If you don't want to lose me, then eat! Be bold and clever!

ADAM
You know that God has warned us clearly and loudly to adhere
To his commandment if we want to remain alive and stay here.
Give me some time to think

EVE
You'll lose me if you don't eat within a blink!
Act more, think less—
Thinking renders action useless . . .

ADAM
(after a moment of hesitation)
Whatever the consequence may be, I will eat
To show you how much I love you, my sweet!

He eats the forbidden fruits. Eve and the fallen angels become relieved and happy.
The sound of a sad music reverberates in the Garden.

ANGLE ON PHANUEL AND RAGUEL.:

Phanuel and Raguel are shocked.

PHANUEL
I can't believe Adam ate the forbidden fruits because of his wife,
Treasuring his wife more than God and choosing death over life!

RAGUEL
It's painful! I wish he didn't! The heart of God will now bleed.
Not only Adam blew it up all, but will pass on his sin to his seed.

AZAZEL
(to the fallen angels)
If, for the sake of that thing located between a woman's thighs
A man boldly disobeys God, his Creator, and consequently dies,
It means that, that thing plays in a man's life an important role,
And that a woman has over a man absolute power and control.

EVE
(to Adam)
Now I know for sure that you love me more than your Maker.

ADAM
(feeling disgraced)
Say not so, Eve. Our fate's intertwined; you're my life's partaker.
I'd rather be down there in hell with you, love,
Than be without you in heaven that is above.

LUCIFER
(to Eve)
Now your husband's talking business, madam.
(turning to Adam)
I'm pleased you're defying God, brave Adam!

EVE
(to Adam)
Do you hear and see anything, dear?
Now, tell me what you see and hear.

ADAM
(observing the area)
Wow! I see plants and angels in great number,
Ugly and hateful, with eyes glowing like ember!

EVE
All these are our new friends, hitherto sealed,
Which the forbidden fruits have now revealed.

LUCIFER
(confronting Adam)
Do I really look ugly and hateful?
Can't you see any better, you fool!
Eve is perplexed.

ADAM
(facing Lucifer)
You're ugly! It's true!
Anyway, who are you!

LUCIFER
Stupid Adam, you're welcome to hell!
You're fallen right now, even as I fell
Disgracefully from high above, cast out of awesome heaven.
You've forfeited your power to me so shamelessly, even
As I relinquished disgracefully my authority in submission
To Michael, for attempting to accomplish a futile mission,
When I tried to usurp God Almighty,
Forgetting that I was minute and petty.

In the beginning, God created me as an angel out of mere fire,
But you were His dream child and the fulfillment of His desire.
He made you alive with His own breath after His own image
And His own likeness, so that He'd be glorified in every age
Through you. You were supposed to worship Him and represent
Him on Earth and Paradise in the distant future and the present.
Now you shall worship me, and you'll be mine.
I'll rule the world in your place. I'll undermine
Your authority. Even your children will be my own,
Poisoned by the nefarious seeds I've maliciously sown.

They'll inherit my rebellious nature, the hatred I did sow
When I rose against God evilly early on in heaven, will grow
In them. They'll hate God unjustly and serve me in madness
By hurting God hard, inflicting on Him unbearable sadness.
You and your wife, Eve, were someday supposed
To enter heaven alive, but because you opposed
God shamefully, misled by your wife, you blew it all up!
O! Miserable Adam, how tragic and bitter is your cup!

EVE
(terrified)
Who are you! We don't know you!

LUCIFER
I'm the snake, you know me. Yes, you do!

EVE
(in tears)
So, you're one of the disgraced creatures!

LUCIFER
You bet . . . you now have my characteristic features.
Therefore, you're both disgraced as I am.
This should be clear to you, Eve and Adam.

ADAM
(regrettably and denying the reality)
I don't know who you are. You were in heaven?
Are you the one who sent to me the evil raven?

LUCIFER
I'm Lucifer the great, the morning star
That used to shine and glitter from afar.
Not only was I in heaven, I was heaven's only glory.
Adventurous, enchanting, and awesome is my story.

AZAZEL
He was next to God even in position and rank.
He's the crown and vertex of creation who sank
To the lowest depth of hell, pulling us all down
To a bottomless pit, losing his glory and crown.

LUCIFER
Oh, Azazel! You're so cruel and gross.
You've to remember I'm still your boss!

AZAZEL
True, you still occupy a higher place
In the principality of the air and space.
But we're equal in shame and disgrace,
Even as Adam and Eve now partake in our lot,
Your irretrievable glory doesn't mean a lot.

ADAM
(to Lucifer)
But by so misleading us, what'll you gain?

LUCIFER
Nothing. I'll only have company in hell. I'll inflict pain
Upon God and man. I will pervert
And divert God's creation; I'll revert

To chaos His perfection, if I can,
And destroy everything and man
To take revenge on God who mercilessly cast
Me out of heaven, making me lose my glory fast.

EVE
Ah! Lucifer, why are you so vicious!

AZAZEL
He turned so vicious and so pernicious
Because he was uncontrollably ambitious.
Oh, my Eve, he made us all evil eons ago
As a result of his vain and unchecked ego.
Because of his maniacal ill desire,
We'll all end up in the Lake of Fire.

EVE
(sobbing)
It's in heaven I want to retire,
I don't want to burn in any fire!

AZAZEL
O! poor Eve, since you defiantly ate
The forbidden fruit, it's now too late!

ADAM
(wrathfully)
Lucifer, you're a liar!

LUCIFER

I speak the truth this time: you're both in a quagmire.
Indeed, God will burn you and us in the Lake of Fire.

Eve continues to wail. Adam is speechless in remorse and sorrow.

AZAZEL
(to Eve)
You're shedding the crocodile's tears,
Eve. You shouldn't have lent your ears
To Lucifer when he was making God a liar,
With false promises, setting your heart afire.
You trusted Lucifer more than God, making him greater.
You, Adam, you obeyed a woman more than your Creator.
In the eyes of God, what you've done is a great sin,
Which on Lucifer and also each other you will pin.

LUCIFER
(to Adam)
Adam, now you're my slave whether you hate
Or love me. You'll never enter heaven's gate;
Yes, that gate God slammed forever behind my back.
You'll go down straight to hell, following in my track!

ADAM

Lucifer, you're the meanest and the repugnant of all,
Though the most powerful and the tallest of the tall!

LUCIFER

Ha! Ha! Ha! I hate you, Adam, your wife, and your God as well!
You've lost Paradise forever! You cannot for long therein dwell!
I hate you and God with a hate, which revolts
And upsets my stomach, and my reasoning bolts.
I've taken over lovely Earth from you with her splendor
To control human affairs with my agenda and calendar!
From now on, the kingdom of Earth is mine, and mine alone,
Till the Kingdom of God comes . . . but your kingdom's gone!

ADAM
(provoked)
What's given to me by God, I'll defend jealously,
I'm not going to fold my arms and stand callously!

LUCIFER
(waving his sword in front of Adam)
Concede defeat, loser! It's over and too late—
You and yours are mine! I decide your fate!
You disobeyed God the moment you obeyed me and fell
From grace. You'll now die and burn in the fire of hell.

EVE
(holding the hand of Adam)
Don't believe him, Adam, we don't have to die—
I've a brilliant idea that dropped from the sky.

ADAM
(with a sad voice in disbelief)
Isn't it too late? What kind of an idea, dear wife?

EVE
Let's live forever by eating of the Tree of Life!

ADAM
(elated by the idea)
What a brilliant idea, brilliant wife!

They rush towards the Tree of Life. However, Lucifer outruns them and stops them, flashing his sword in their faces.

LUCIFER
O, dumb husband and stupid, brilliant wife,
I won't allow you to eat of the Tree of Life!

ADAM
Lucifer, you can't stop us whatsoever! It's none of your business!

LUCIFER
You're now my business! Everything you do gives me uneasiness!
You're a sinner just like me. So, I won't allow you to live forever!
It should be clear—you won't live eternally anymore, whatsoever!

The Holy Trinity appear with their archangels. Archangel Michael has two lambs with him. Adam and Eve hide from the Holy Trinity.

CHRIST
(to Lucifer)
So, you struck Adam with the deadly rock you hurled,
Which we foresaw before the foundations of the world.

LUCIFER
(bragging, yet trembling with fear)
You bet! I did it indeed!
I was destined to succeed.
Those people you've created for your divine
Glory are no more yours. They're now mine.

They chose to trust and obey me more.
Than you. They'll be mine, therefore.
As you are an upright God, you'll banish man from Paradise
To his demise, as you banished me mercilessly to my demise.

CHRIST
You said it right. I'm impartial to all my creatures.
I punish them equally when they become breachers,
Transgressing my laws and statutes in defiance,
Desiring equality with me, united in evil affiance.
It's clear I'm a God of justice as much as I'm of mercy,
I'm a God of punishment as much as I'm of clemency.
God looks for Adam and Eve.

HOLY TRINITY
Where are you, Eve . . . Adam?
Come out! It's me, I AM!

ADAM AND EVE
(almost stuttering)
Lord, we're embarrassed to face
You. We're naked . . . in disgrace . . .

HOLY TRINITY
How do you know you're naked? Did
You eat of the tree that I did forbid?

Adam and Eve cover their private parts with leaves and approach God. They are shaking in fear and shame. Lucifer follows them.

ADAM
(pointing at Eve)
This very woman called Eve you gave me for wife
Enticed me to eat it saying, "It'll change your life . . ."

EVE
The serpent enticed me and made me fall,
Saying, "You'll be like God, knowing all."

LUCIFER
(with a malicious smile)
I sowed in her a poisonous seed.
Yes, it's my work! I did succeed!

CHRIST
(to Lucifer)
Move away for a moment.
We'll discuss our judgment.

Lucifer moves away a bit further from God and sits on a rock, eavesdropping on what the Holy Trinity discuss.

ADAM
I now know why you did not give me a wife
Right away. You knew she'd destroy my life.
She who has come out of my own self has now become my enemy.
When Lucifer tempted me, I resisted. It's through her he got me!
O, my God, I wish you didn't splinter my bone
To make her! I wish I remained eternally alone!

CHRIST
(sadly)
I gave you freewill. You chose your wife
Over your Maker and over eternal life.
You rejected God for a vicious ambition. Hence,
Beloved son, you have to suffer the consequence.

HOLY SPIRIT
(also sadly, to Adam and Eve)
Ah, Adam and Eve! The two of you brought a curse
Upon yourselves today, consequential and adverse:
Ah, children in our image, you died today spiritually,
Also inflicting upon yourselves physical death, actually.

Father God speaks loudly to the Holy Spirit and Christ, so that Adam and Eve hear clearly.

FATHER GOD
Adam and Eve have committed a high treason.
They should be punished by death for this reason.
I regret we created them with loving kindness in our image.
Let's rid of them right now before they inflict more damage.
In fact, just like Lucifer, they deserve to go straight to hell
Without mercy, since they've learned from him to rebel.

ADAM AND EVE
(crying and repenting)
Forgive us, God, though Lucifer exerted on us a pressure,
We've to admit we're guilty! Our own sin has no measure!
We're so sorry we committed treason
Behind your back, for no good reason!

They sob in repentance. The Trinity discuss the future of Adam and Eve.

CHRIST
(making sure that Adam and Eve hear Him)
Oh, no Father, we agreed together to make
Adam. And I made him for our joy's sake.
He fell because of our enemy's evil intention,
Sadly, with erroneous and false contention,
Aimed at disrupting the divine plan
We had designed for the chosen man.
Why should we please our formidable and vengeful adversary
By killing them? To serve justice, I will die myself if necessary,
In their place. They've repented profoundly. We shouldn't destroy
Them. Being in our image, they're objects of our hope, love, and joy.

HOLY SPIRIT
O! Beloved, you've done nothing wrong to deserve
Death. Man's sentence we should for man reserve.

CHRIST
I intercede for man—let my own death restore
Man to us, despite the sorrow I'll have in store.
I'll be crucified in mockery wearing a thorny crown.
Because I love man so much, I will lay my life down,
So that death, which has entered the world as a consequence
Of one man's sin, is eliminated by another's redemption; hence,
Balancing in due course the equilibrium of justice,
Which otherwise remains unfairly tilted for all to notice.
As I'd vowed before we made Adam long ago
To save him when he falls because of his ego,
I've to die willingly even though I'll endure
Unfathomable pain and sorrow, for sure.

FATHER GOD & HOLY SPIRIT
May it be as you wish, Amen! Amen!
Die and save them, we too, love men!
Five and half days will pass in heaven, 5,500 years
On Earth; men will multiply in number, and tears

Will mix with blood, violence being man's behavior.
When darkness eclipses Earth, she'll cry for a savior,
And you'll take a physical body from a child of Adam,
Be born a true Light unto men, exposing Satan's sham,
Restoring what he would steal, destroy, and kill,
Granting life abundantly, dying of your own will.

HOLY SPIRIT
(to Adam and Eve)
In the past, our grace and close presence
To you, protected you from pain in essence.
Now, there's a big chasm between us caused by sin.
It's only our beloved Son who'll bridge it and win
Back the power and glory you've lost to Lucifer.
You're now in a real death row and would suffer
The consequence if our Son doesn't die to bear your sorrow
And snatch you by His mercy out of that dreadful death row.
No man can set you free, for every man is a criminal hence.
Only our sinless Son can get you out of your death sentence.

He's willing to shed His precious blood
To save you, letting it flow like flood.
Meantime, you've to cover your sins—it'll suffice
To sacrifice animals till our Son's actual sacrifice.
In other words, until our beloved Son dies lovingly in your stead,
Animal blood will cover your sins though you're spiritually dead.

ANGLE ON LUCIFER EAVESDROPPING INTENSELY.

CHRIST
(to Adam)
As it's through a woman you brought into the world sin,
I, too, will come through a woman into the world and win
You your salvation when the time draws near
For my birth on Earth at the appointed year.
Whereas you brought death eating from a tree,
I'll die on the wood of a tree to set you free.
They'll nail me cruelly to a wood and pierce
Me with a spear . . . my enemies will be fierce!
You've polluted your blood by a fatal sin. It's now corrupt.
Your children will inherit it and pass it on. I've to interrupt
This vicious cycle and renew the sinful blood,
By my sinless blood after I die and let it flood . . .

When I wear flesh, if your children believe in me and become mine,
I'll replace their corrupted, Satanic bloodline with my bloodline.
So that your children may know there's life in me even after death,
I'll raise myself on the third day after I breathe my last breath.
Since I'll die on behalf of your children and yourselves, when
I die, it'll certainly be as though you've all died with me. And then
When I rise from death, it'll be as though you've all victoriously risen.
When I ascend to heaven, you'll ascend with me for the same reason.
And when I sit at the right hand of God after I land
In heaven, it's as though you've sat on His right hand.

FATHER GOD
(to Christ)
Son, let's sacrifice two lambs right now and cover
Them with their blood and skins until you take over.
Later, we'll advise them how to offer animal sacrifice
For the remission of sins, if they will follow our advice.

CHRIST
(to Michael)
Michael, kill the two lambs, burn their meat as a sacrifice.
Until I shed my own blood, animals' should suffice.

Michael does as commanded by his Lord. Christ covers Adam and Eve with the bloody skins of the animals, symbolizing the temporary covering of their sins by animal blood.

ANGLE ON LUCIFER AND HIS ANGELS.

LUCIFER
(to his angels)
Hey! Imitating God, I'll demand in the future from Adam's
Children to sacrifice for me human beings instead of lambs.
That way, I'll pervert God's pure plan and pretend
I'm God, so that it's me they'll worship and tend.

AZAZEL
I'll be satisfied with animals. I'll teach humans witchcraft skill
To ask them to kill me animals, which I don't doubt they'll kill.

LUCIFER
We all wish we were humans owning the human body.
Since we can't have one, possessing one is the remedy,
By sneaking in, in disguise or even breaking in under cover,
To be a roommate first and later on completely take over.

I overheard God say He will get a body from Adam's seed.
He's lucky. He might as well keep the body forever indeed.
After that, God will be both human and divine.
Since I'm the cause, the credit should be mine!

ANNANEL
It's weird that such a thought runs through your head.
Tell me how He could keep the body if He's really dead?

LUCIFER
Did you hear Him saying He'll rise from the dead
And return with the body to His former Godhead?

AZAZEL
Should that happen, we will lose the battle,
And become as worthless as a rotten spittle.

SEMAZYA
(to Lucifer)
You wanted to hurt God. Your intent was devilish.
Yet, you'll help Him greater things to accomplish.

LUCIFER
(suddenly excited)
I'll have God Himself killed. I made it big time!
God will be punished for my sins and crime!
I'll yet pervert and pollute Adam's descendants
With spiritual filth, when they multiply like ants,
Causing strife, lies, wars, carnage, jealousy, violence,
Selfishness, contempt, sexual perversion, and insolence.
I will replace human joy with mourning and teeth gnashing,
Everything and everyone trampling over evilly and trashing,
As I did in the past, with the other civilizations and races,
Utterly destroying them, annihilating them without traces,
Upsetting God and striking Him with lightening of grief,
Until the day He burns me in hell to finally get His relief.

AZAZEL
Did you do everything you did by yourself? Come on!

LUCIFER
Of course, I owe all of you every battle and war I won.

FATHER GOD
(to Adam and Eve)
You'll surely live long parenting children. In every time and age,
Your descendants should stick together bonded in holy marriage.
They shouldn't marry unbelievers who're outside their members,
Lest they stray away surely, get lost, and wane just like embers.
We will give you all the details of our commandments
Later, including the offers and sacrifices for atonements.
Your descendants will be our
Priests for ages, and tower . . .

Father God waves His hand at Lucifer and the fallen angels to come near Him, and they do as ordered.

(to Eve)
For attempting to be our equal in knowledge and faculty,
Obeying vicious Satan, you'll bear children with difficulty.
You'll be utterly dependent on your husband
Like man depends on oasis in a desert sand.
(to Adam)
And you, Adam, for loving, trusting and obeying your wife
More than us, you shall toil and sweat, leading a hard life,
and losing Paradise. Because of you Earth shall be cursed
Yielding thorns. It'll be in tears, blood, and agony immersed.

(to Lucifer)
And you shall be called a serpent. I'll establish enmity afresh
Between Eve's and your seeds when the Word becomes flesh.
Your seeds are your followers, your obedient servants
Who'll destroy Earth and life to appease your evil wants.
He'll bruise your head, and you'll bruise His heels in retaliation.
His heels are His followers that follow Him in self-humiliation.
You'll entice evil people to wound His feet with nails and crucify
Him. He'll crush your head after His resurrection to redeem, justify
And free humanity from your old and cruel bondage,
By granting men eternal life, nullifying your damage.
(to Adam and Eve)
Since posing and speaking like an animal, Satan the nefarious
Beguiled you, we prohibit animals to speak to man. The various
Animals too shall be expelled from Paradise and Eden together
With you two, whether the animals wear skin or even feather.

Jesus weeps.

FATHER GOD
Son, don't weep, please!
Have peace! Be at ease!

CHRIST
Ah! . . . I just remembered the day we banished
Lucifer, when our life with him was finished.
And now it's Adam and Eve's turn to lose grace,
And likewise, be banished in disgrace from our face.

HOLY SPIRIT
They got what they deserved,
Dear Son. Justice is served.

FATHER GOD
(To Michael and Gabriel)
Michael, expel these two rebels to Earth from Paradise!
Cherubs, you've to guard the Tree of Life. Otherwise
They would dare eat of its fruits and live forever and ever
In their sins, causing us pain from which we can't recover.
Send them back to Elda, the place of their origin!
Make sure they never set foot on this holy region!

CHRIST
(to Michael and Gabriel)
If, in their sinful state, Adam and Eve live even like us forever,
They'll be lost forever. I can't die and redeem them whatsoever,
Which is why you should fiercely prevent the man and his wife
From living in sinfulness forever by eating of the Tree of Life.
So, assign cherubs with flaming swords to guard without delay
The Tree of Life. Paradise is sealed till I die for man someday.

LUCIFER
(to his angels)
Ah! I wish I didn't prevent them from eating of the Tree of Life!
I didn't know any better. Now God will save Adam and his wife.

Adam and Eve cry.

ADAM AND EVE
Have mercy, Lord God! We conjure you, have mercy!

FATHER GOD
Only through sacrifice will you have mercy and clemency.

Fikre Tolossa, Ph.D.

HOLY SPIRIT
(to the angels)
Yes, the two were formed from earth on the planet Earth.
Therefore, banish them to Earth, the place of their birth!

The Holy Trinity leave.

LUCIFER
(to his angels)
Hurrah! Hurrah! I did it! Yes! I did it again,
Inflicting on God and man unbearable pain!
I, Lucifer, heaven's glory, creation's apex, the morning star!
Are there any crafty ones like myself? None are! Who can bar
Me to do what I like? I maneuver the great, I manipulate the small.
Most of God's creatures are now mine! Indeed, I'm adored by all
In all the worlds. I will cause God to die and taste that bitter cup!
After that, I'll plunge Him into Hades, as He cast me from high up!
What's more revenge than kill God in such a retaliatory infection,
Creating a chasm between Him and man, object of His affection!
Oh, friends, there'll be no more remarkable day in world history
Like the day I'll have God killed. That'll be my greatest victory!
Oh, I'll be so high! Oh, I'll feel proud and good
On the day I see Almighty God nailed to a wood!

AZAZEL
Oh, shortsighted Satan, don't you get it? The day God is killed
Is the day you'll lose it all, because, by His own death He willed
To snatch man and your power out of your feeble hand regardless
Of your bragging, and to crush your head and render you useless!
There's nothing you can do lest He wills, as He's in control.
He'll use you to accomplish His mission and reach His goal.
Forgetting the thorns, when you focus on the rose,
You'll lose it all, not looking beyond your nose!

LUCIFER
Azazel, aren't you on my side? Are you trying to hurt my pride?

AZAZEL
I'm on the side of the truth at least once, leaving your pride aside.

Michael, Gabriel, Raphael, and Raguel drive out of Paradise Adam and Eve, as well as all animals, Lucifer, and his evil angels. Sadly, the holy angels expel the wailing couples from Paradise in the same way they had cast out of heaven the rebellious angels ages ago. Six cherubs run to the Tree of Life and guard it with rotating swords of flames. A dozen cherubs guard the gates of Paradise itself to open them only after 5,533 years when the Word Christ becomes human (Jesus), to keep His promise to Adam and Eve to die willingly at the age of

33, to go to Hades in the spirit to reach the souls of Adam and Eve and their children, to preach the Good Gospel there, and to take them to Paradise triumphantly.

FADE OUT.

THE END.

The story will continue in *Promise Fulfilled,* the sequel to *Heaven To Eden.*

Review Requested:

If you loved this book, would you please provide a review at Amazon.com?

CPSIA information can be obtained
at www.ICGtesting.com
Printed in the USA
LVOW03s1737230117
521875LV00004BA/289/P